Good and Faithful Servants

The Story of the Sisters of the People in the Presbyterian Church of Wales

By Jean Cannon

CONTENTS

Pages

Acknowledgements | 1

Introduction | 2

1. Early Beginnings | 3
2. Early Days of the Sisters of the People | 10
3. Slum Stories from the Diary of Martha Jones Sister of the People | 22
4. Treborth Preventative Home | 33
5. Kingswood – Treborth Rescue and Preventative Homes | 38
6. Help and Hindrances | 50
7. Blood, Sweat, Toil and Tears – Sister's Reports | 55
8. A New Vision for a New Era | 63
9. New Beginnings – North Wales | 67
10. New Beginnings – South Wales | 74
11. Warts and All | 85
12. Long Serving Sisters of the People | 90
13. Champions of the Cause | 100
14. What Shall We Say to These Things? | 107

An Index of Sisters of the People 1903 – 1993 | 114

References | 116

Bibliography | 122

ACKNOWLEDGEMENTS

I acknowledge, with gratitude, the quiet encouragement and guidance of Dr D Eryl Davies, who, in so many ways, is a giant of the Faith.

I am also grateful for the interest and encouragement of Fiona Steward, Women's Pastoral Leader at Heath Evangelical Church.

Pastor John Funnell, Noddfa, Abersychan, was very generous with information for input into the final chapter of the book. His work in Abersychan is truly inspirational.

Thanks also to Alex at Abersychan for allowing me to include part of his testimony.

I am particularly indebted to the kindness of the staff of Llandaff North and Gabalfa Hub, who allowed me to sit over many, many days in a wonderfully comfortable and warm room, whilst I read through fifty years of denominational journals.

Thanks also to Bethan Jenkins for translating material from Welsh to English, and to Ceri Lord and Pauline Beckington for typing the manuscript.

INTRODUCTION

The contribution of women throughout many aspects of modern history, secular and religious, for various reasons, is either sparsely recorded, or not recorded at all.

Vast volumes have been written about our greatest men; but very little has been written about our best women. The thrilling, and at times heroic story of the Sisters of the People of the Presbyterian Church of Wales, has been largely lost in the memory of Christians in Wales, and is probably completely unknown in broader Christendom. Someone has said "women were the golden thread in the garment of Welsh Presbyterianism"

This isn't a book only for women; it's a book about women – but it's a book for everyone – to encourage both men and women in their faith.

For some unknown reason, I felt burdened to record the work and legacy of the Sisters of the People.

Researching for this book has presented some challenges because there is no substantive or specific archival material attributed to the Sisters of the People. References to the Sisters of the People and their exemplary work are scattered, like needles in haystacks, amongst individual church records, denominational journals, newspaper reporting, Connexional records and various other secondary sources. Thus I have attempted to piece together and record their inspiring legacy. I realise that I may not have found every needle hidden in every haystack that I searched. Therefore it is possible that a valuable service remains undiscovered and unrecorded in this book, and particularly if the service was of short duration, and for this I am truly sorry.

I have found the task of researching and writing a huge privilege, and both thrilling and energising; and it has revitalised my Christian faith.

I trust this book will be a blessing and inspiration to both men and women who read of the wonderful works of God through the amazing Sisters of the People.

Chapter One – Early Beginnings

> "I am persuaded that a bird could as soon fly with one wing as the Church of God can evangelise the great centres of the population without Christ-possessed women to go in and out among the suffering poor. There is a work that no-one can do for Christ but them." [1]

These are the words of Rev. John Pugh, the founder of the Cardiff Evangelistic Movement (later known as the Forward Movement). These words were the launch pad for the formation of the group of women known as 'Sisters of the People' of the Calvinistic Methodists (later, Presbyterian Church Of Wales). They brought the compassion and love of Christ to families blighted by poverty, immorality and the curse of intemperance. They were able to enter situations that were not open to male missionaries. They worked tirelessly and selflessly to bring the gospel to all. Their work included children's work, visitation, prison work, tract distribution and open-air witness, work amongst women in all aspects, and so much more. They worked long and hard, under very difficult circumstances. Some were in sole charge of Forward Movement Halls and worked alone and did everything. They often lived amongst the people they worked amongst; thus enjoying few earthly comforts. Their work for the Kingdom of God was truly amazing – and this is their story.

Sisters of the People was not a title used exclusively by the Forward Movement of the Calvinistic Methodists (later Presbyterian Church of Wales). It was used by other denominations for similar work; namely by the Wesleyan Methodists and the Primitive Methodists. The term 'Forward Movement' was coined by Hugh Price Hughes of the Wesleyan Methodists. The term was later used by the Baptists and the Congregationalists in the 1890s. The Forward Movement of the Calvinistic Methodists was an evangelical mission to reach the vast numbers of working-class people who had migrated into the cities in search of work in the steel works, the docks, the railways and other work. Many lived in slums in abject poverty and were victims of immorality and the 'demon drink.'

However, in 1889, Rev. John Pugh became the minister of Clifton Street Presbyterian Church, Cardiff. He had previously had powerful ministries at Tredegar and Pontypridd. John Pugh soon built a strong congregation at Clifton Street, but he carried a great burden. He saw that the religious provision for Cardiff was woefully inadequate and the majority of people were ignorant of their great spiritual needs. John Pugh saw a great need for an awakening amongst the churches to the great spiritual and welfare needs of the masses, and the power of the gospel to transform these lives.

Acting on the great burden he felt, John Pugh persuaded Seth Joshua to bring his marquee to a site at East Moors, Cardiff (one of the poorest areas of Cardiff); and it was there, on Sunday 3rd May 1891, where the first tent mission was held of what would first become the Cardiff Evangelistic Movement, and then later, the Forward Movement was birthed.

In July 1891, John Pugh wrote:

> "GO FORWARD" – These are days of advance. That the churches have caught, to some degree, the spirit of the times, is evidenced by the readiness with which the name of 'Forward Movement' is given to any special advance on new lines in Christian work. We cannot but see in all this the finger of God, and that the Captain of the Lord's hosts is in many ways repeating the command given of old, "Speak unto the children of Israel, that they go forward." [2]

It was at the meeting of the General Assembly of the Presbyterian Church of Wales at Morriston on June the 22nd – 24th 1891 that this denomination formed the Church Extension and Mission Work Society, to be commonly known as the Forward Movement; and the Cardiff Evangelistic Movement came under the control, influence and auspices of the denomination.

In January 1892, John Pugh wrote under the heading, 'An earnest appeal for great united action to win Wales for Christ'. It is in this article that John Pugh gave a strong indication that his vision for the Forward Movement had a specific and vital role for women. He wrote:

> "Our Christian women must be more and more utilised for Christian work – the Christian women of Wales have never yet been taught or encouraged to do what they can for Jesus Christ. They have been kept largely in the background and we are suffering today in consequence. If this latent force of Christian womanhood in our churches were only once called out, it would make the kingdom of darkness tremble. Awake! awake! ye Christian mothers and daughters of Wales and go forth in the strength of God and capture your country from the drunkenness and the

vice, and the worldliness and superstition which now threatens us on every hand. If you cannot go to India to help your sin cursed sisters there, try and do all you can for your native land. Be up then and doing, for the night will come when your opportunity will be over." [3]

John Pugh's burden for an active positive role for women in the work of the Forward Movement was reinforced by encouraging examples he saw working so well in other denominations. John Pugh was a great friend of William Ross of Cowcaddens, Glasgow, who utilised Sisters of the People, some of whom were nurses and some of whom worked mainly with the prostitutes in the city (Atgofion am John Pugh, p37). William Ross also utilised the Theory of the Pioneer Mission. The inspiration for this came from the Slum Sisters work of the Salvation Army. The theory of the Pioneer Missions was that Christian women should be placed in a house in the centre of a slum area, where they would provide a Christian household as an example, visit and help out the neighbours when needed, and also hold regular meetings in the Mission house. They were instructed to keep their work within the immediate vicinity, and even with these instructions in place, the pioneer missionaries had several hundred people they needed to evangelise and visit.

In 1893, John Pugh took his daughter to Cowcaddens, Glasgow. She explained why:

> "He wanted me to see the Sisters of the People at work there. It seems that William Ross had spoken one day to a poor lady about her soul, who, looking pathetically in his face had replied, "Oh, Mr Ross, if you were as hungry as I am you wouldn't have time to think about your soul." That woman's face and answer left such an impression on Rev. Ross' tender nature that was never to go away. He was deeply challenged by the Lord's attitude to such 'When he saw the multitudes He had compassion on them." [4]

Lord Overton, a great Scottish philanthropist provided the finance for six experienced Christian nurses to go among the poor of Cowcaddens, and six Sisters of the People, who had been taught in the Bible Institute, Glasgow, who in their turn went out at night to contact the prostitutes. These dedicated women lived among the people in the crowded closes.

Anne Pugh remembered;

> "One night I dressed in Sisters' uniform for safety and went with Sister Jessie on her nightly round. As we walked through the streets, I saw sights that made my blood boil with anger. I should have felt compassion and sympathy for the women. Maybe it wasn't right, but the feelings that were uppermost were those of shame and fear.
> Sister Jessie noticed a girl stood in a doorway of a house, touting for work. Sister Jessie went up to her and said,
> "Here is the last flower I have left and would you like to have it?"
> The girl in the doorway took the simple gift and replied,
> "It's been a long time since anyone gave me a flower," and then she added, "It's been a long time since a respectable girl even spoke to me at all."
> Sister Jessie looked at her and said, "You're not very happy are you? Can I do anything for you?"
> "No, there's nothing that can be done."
> Sister Jessie said, "There might be. Think about it – anyway, you know where to find me, don't you? Come in to see me and let me be your friend."
> We returned to Sister's room in the Close and spoke of the great need for a work which could prevent what was going on. The doorbell rang. There was the girl with the flower in her hand.
> She said, "When you asked me if you could do anything for me, I said you couldn't. But you said perhaps you could and invited me. Well, I've come now. I want you to help me. It was the white flower that you gave me that made me come here. It wouldn't leave me alone." [4]

John Pugh was also influenced by Rev. Hugh Price Hughes, a Wesleyan Methodist who founded the West London Mission, who worked in the midst of the slum areas where social needs were great.

Dorothea Price Hughes, who wrote her father's biography, stated;

> "He wanted a band of large hearted, sensible, capable Christian women to be a centre of service and help in the great whirlpool of West London slum life – not to look down on miserable and distraught humanity from

a superior height, but to place themselves by the side of the sinful and sad. He wanted them to be 'Sisters of the People,' the name which was afterwards adopted. [5]

John Pugh pondered all these things in his heart, and in 1894, 'The Women's Branch' of the Forward Movement was formed, supported by three hundred women, who met at an Association at Llanrwst.

In August 1894, the following article was written;

> 'Sisters of the People' Department.
> The Forward Movement has much pleasure in bringing to the notice of our readers the new Department, recently formed called the 'Sisters of the People' Department.
> The reason given for its formation is that 'during years of aggressive work in what has been termed, 'Darker Cardiff' and other dark spots, we have had forced upon us not only the deplorable condition of hundreds of homes, but also certain phases of evil and suffering, which male missionaries are utterly unable to cope with.'

The objects of the department are:

1. To bring the light of God's salvation into those wretched homes where its blessings have never entered.
2. To deliver the inmates, as far as possible, from the curse of intemperance, which is the cause of so much misery, and to instil into them the principles of thrift and cleanliness.
3. To relieve temporal suffering and want to the utmost of our ability, by wisely administering to their needs.
4. To establish a Temporary Home for friendless and fallen girls.
5. To get young Christian women of promise trained for the department in some special Training Home established for the same, until we are able to establish one for ourselves.
6. To arrange for some of these trained Sisters to visit towns or districts where their services may be required to assist the churches to reach the lapsed masses, and thus help to reduce the present great army of non-chapel and church goers to a minimum.

This Department, if taken up earnestly by the women of our churches, throughout North and South Wales, can be made a means of great blessing to all our towns and villages, as well as a source of strength to the Forward Movement proper. It will supply our women members with a simple and effective organisation, by means of which they can render invaluable service to our churches everywhere. [6]

John Pugh had noticed how the Roman Catholic churches, the Anglican churches and the Salvation Army were using their dedicated, able women. He felt that there were within the Calvinistic Methodist denomination many similar resolute and able women, who would be invaluable to their churches and to those unfortunate and despised by society. John Pugh felt it was fine to ask educated and privileged women to consecrate their gifts in the service of the church. They would do the kind of work that others could not. The word 'Sister' was used in human and democratic terms, without any ecclesiastical significance. He wanted an army of Christian women, who were able, wise and with big hearts to be the centre of service and help in the big industrial towns of Wales. They would not look down on pitiful humanity from some superior pinnacle, but come alongside them in their sinful, pitiful state. He wanted them to be the Sisters of the People. [7]

Whilst many helpful 'Women's Branches' were set up in North and South Wales, it was not until 1903 at the Amlwch General Assembly, that the Women's Branch was placed on a broad and firm denominational basis. It had taken a 'slow moving church' five years to formalise the 'Women's Branch.'

Pugh put forward a proposal to the Amlwch General Assembly that a start be made by placing a Sister of the People at Saltmead, Cardiff. Pugh's proposal was supported by a searing speech from Rev. Barker, one of Pugh's most zealous and original evangelists, who worked in notorious Saltmead, Cardiff. Members of the Assembly sat appalled as the wraps were taken off life in an area of notoriety in Cardiff.

Barker said;

> "From three to four hundred fallen women reside in my District. There are more than one hundred houses empty because they have been

occupied for immoral purposes. I know girls going straight from the Sabbath school to the streets, and thirty of these have gone since I am in Saltmead. These girls are expected to adopt this life even by some of the parents." [8]

That settled the question. The Assembly, possibly with a sense of shame for their short-sightedness and lack of the spirit of Christian endeavour, unanimously passed that a Bible woman be appointed for protective work at the Saltmead centre of the Forward Movement.

John Pugh was full of gratitude and he acquainted the Directors of the Assembly that on Hugh Price Hughes' own admission, the success of his work in the West end of London was due more to the work of the Sisters of the People than to anything else.

Chapter Two – Early Days of the Sisters of the People

The Early Sisters of the People

Sister Lloyd
Sister Alison Jones
Sister Eileen Walker
Sister Church
Sister Thomas (widow of Rev. J. Thomas)
Sister Rose Carter
Sister Hill
Sister Gertrude Davies
Sister Sarah Jones
Sister Elizabeth Jones
Sister Kate Jones
Sister Ellen Watkins

Thus, the first Sister of the People to be appointed in 1903 was to Saltmead, Cardiff, under the auspices of the Forward Movement, and she was Sister L M Lloyd, and here is her testimony from the Torch, January 1909;

> "In giving a brief summary of my connection with the Women's Branch from its commencement up to the present, I experience a deep thankfulness to God who led me into contact with this part of His vineyard. Well do I remember the day, in June 1903, when sitting with a group of girls in training at Liverpool for God's wide mission field, discussing plans for the long summer vacation that was at hand, I suddenly thought, Well! I will write to Dr Pugh, though I knew next to nothing about him, and ask him to allow me to visit South Wales and spend a few weeks there to see the work. I sat down and wrote a short note, directed it to Dr Pugh, and asked Him who knew everything about me to guide the issue thereof. By return came the answer, written in a way characteristic of the kind, gracious heart of the writer, telling me of

the great need of women workers in the town of Cardiff; also stating that my application had supplied the missing link he wanted in the chain of events to convince him that at last the time was fully ripe to start what he so longed to see – a Women's Branch of the Forward Movement. Official permission was asked for at the General Assembly held in the course of the following week. It was granted: and shortly afterwards I came to South Wales to see the work and the Centre where I was destined to get my first experience.

A wonderful and blessed experience it proved to be! For two years I was privileged to work under the direction of the Rev. B. G. Barker; and who better than he could give a new worker the right kind of work. It is not all of those who have wide experience in doing the Master's work that are great enough to be humble enough to lay bare their experience for the sake of helping on a girl worker as he did. And may I be allowed to state that the Women's Branch owes him a debt of gratitude.

The work of a Sister at Saltmead meant going in and out of the homes of the people, endeavouring to enter into their joys and sorrows, gradually winning their confidence and trust, and being enabled in that way to understand the strange standpoint from which some of them look at life, and therefore to help them. Many other things beside visiting is expected from a Sister, and her life becomes soon a very busy one, brim-full of interest. Strange requests are brought to her. A mother will come, bringing along a daughter whom she has failed to manage, expecting the Sister to make an angel of the girl at once. Then comes a women – a poor downtrodden creature, requesting the Sister to call at her house at a certain time, in order to catch the husband in, so as to give him, as his wife expresses it, 'A good talking to.' Neither is it a rare experience for a Sister to be compelled to listen whilst some fellow pours into her ears his difficulties with whom he refers to as 'That woman of mine.' And many a time during those two precious years at Saltmead I had to enter a drunken, riotous home, in order to do what I could to stop the husband and wife from beating one another with pokers, or any other dangerous articles they could lay their hands on. One quarter of what a Sister is expected to do in a district like that cannot be recorded on paper. Sufficient is said, perhaps, in order to give the reader some idea." [1]

By March 1905, Sister Lloyd was joined by Sister Alison Jones (based at Grangetown) and Sister Walker (based at East Moors). [2]

In 1906, Sister Church was posted to Pontypool [3] and Sister Thomas (widow of the Rev. John Thomas, Abercarn) was posted to Malpas Road, Newport. [4]

By 1908, Sister Rose Carter had been posted to Barry [5] and Sister Hill had been posted to Neath. [6]

Finances became a severe limiting factor for the expansion of the Sisters of the People work. The Women's Branch of the Presbyterian Church of Wales (Forward Movement) were tasked with raising the funds to support both the work of the Sisters of the People and the Preventative and Rescue Home (Kingswood Treborth).

In 1910, the treasurer of the Women's Branch writes as follows;

> "It is well to be reminded of the central place the Lord Jesus Christ occupies in our faith. He is the centre of the Gospel. Assurance of this gives buoyancy midst disappointments, and courage when face to face with foe. We were driven to our knees during the last few weeks. Our resources have been exhausted. With a heavy overdraft in the bank, and nothing in hand to pay salaries for our seven faithful Sisters of the People, and forty in Kingswood – Treborth home He has touched the hearts of His people, and replies are flowing in as a result of the subjoined appeal to our English churches." [7]

During a conference at Llandrindod, organised by the Women's Branch for reports from the Sisters of the People, but also for time to meditate on the deeper things of the Spirit and to be fed by the Word, visitors joined from all over Wales. So powerful and challenging were the reports from the Sisters of the People, and so great the need for financial support, that many removed their jewellery and put it in the collecting boxes in order to support the work. [8]

The financial difficulties of the Forward Movement were never far away, and in 1908, a Pastor wrote a letter to the editor of Y Goleuad as follows;

"To the editor of Y Goleuad
A Sister of the People.
Sir, years ago the needs of the lapsed in South Wales weighed heavily on the soul of John Pugh. He risked his all on behalf of the God he loved, and the people whom he wished would also love the same Father. Brother Pugh started a movement that has blessed Wales and infused new life into the Calvinistic Methodist Church. But whatever man is able to accomplish, he cannot do his work well alone and this the leaders of the Movement discovered so they started a new 'order' in the church. Brother Pugh and his friends created another order – the Sisters of the People. The Sisters of the People are few in number, and those who are working do the work not because they love ease or money but because they love the Lord. The pay is meagre, the work is arduous and discouraging but the joy of leading souls to the Saviour compensates for all. Daughters of godly homes, firmly rooted in the love of God, here is a splendid chance to give.

Had the committee of the Forward Movement money, they could do greater things for God. It is chiefly among the degraded that the Sisters of the People work. There is a Rescue and Preventative home in Cardiff to which, cases, are sent occasionally. The Sisters of the People may have to attend the Police Court. They visit the mean streets to read and pray with the inmates. They have to reprimand them for their folly and sin and have the pleasure of leading souls from darkness to light. The work varies from district to district but the general principles remain the same. The Sisters of the People visit places, where evangelists, for specific reasons cannot go. They visit the sick and afflicted, and their duty lies chiefly with the stranger outside the gate. They seek in the highways and hedges for guests for the King. The work is carried out by the Calvinistic Methodist Church but the church feels the burden to be heavy. A debt of £80,000 on the halls of the Movement hampers the work….Who will help?"   Pastor [9]

The vision for a Training Institute

Appropriate training for the Sisters of the People was an initial problem, as part of John Pugh's vision was to have a Training School where young Christian women could train in Wales for work amongst the poor, instead of having to go to England or Scotland for training. The Christian Standard, June 1892, outlines John Pugh's vision for a Training Home and the difficulties encountered in trying to realise the vision for 'a place where theological students and earnest young Christian men and women might have some practical knowledge of mission and pastoral work'. But to John Pugh's great sorrow and disappointment, his appeal for help to do this found no practical response, except from the late Principal Davies of Trevecca College. This is the more amazing, when no part of his plan of campaign had been more commended than his idea of the Training Home. A suitable site was in view, and a suitable Training Home could be built for £500. A great friend of the Forward Movement suggested that as one of the great halls was to be called 'The Memorial Hall' in honour of the late friend of all good work, David Davies, Llandinam, so this Training Home should be called 'Principal Davies' Training Home' in memory of the deep interest he took in it, and of the generosity he manifested towards it. It was evident to all that John Pugh was in dead earnest about it, and that he determined to give the Forward Movement a Training Home, but in the Providence of God it was not to be, as John Pugh died in 1907, and the Training Home was never built.

The Training Institute was planned to be next to the Pierce Hall (the Sunday School room of the Crwys Forward Movement Church, Cardiff). The sketch below from 1906 shows the plan for the Training Institute. [10]

Crwys School Hall and Proposed Training Home for Sisters of the People.

Courtesy of the Presbyterian Church of Wales, Torch Magazine Sept 1906

Here are a few heartwarming and challenging reports from Sisters of the People in the very early days of the work, and also recognition and commendation of their work by Ministers and members of the Forward Movement.

Report from Sister Alison Jones, Merthyr

Here is a report from Sister Alison Jones – The work of a Sister of the People at Merthyr (Torch Aug 1909); [11]

> "Sister Alison gave a short account of her own conversion in a Forward Movement Hall in Newport, and then showed that it was as St Paul says, "By grace we are saved." Grace was, she said, something more than love, for it was love that humbles itself (God humbled Himself that He might present to us eternal life) and, like gold, the more grace is handled the brighter it shines. That was her answer to the question, "Why bother about prisoners?" One poor woman has made 106 appearances in the

Police court, yet there is still hope for her. Some of God's jewels are to be found among the vilest in this town if we will only look for them. Sixteen women and girls have been rescued and lodged in homes since Sister Alison arrived in Merthyr, and they are all doing well. Some more examples from Sister Alison's work:

1. A young girl in London made up her mind to come to Wales. One night, just as she was, she left her friends and tramped all the way, sleeping on doorsteps etc. nearly the whole time. She came into contact with our work in Merthyr and is now doing well in a situation.
2. One morning when visiting the cells, I saw a poor girl who had evidently seen better days. She was wearing a locket photo of her sister (a nurse in a London hospital). Her parents had paid £50 to have her taught her trade. She fell and had to leave. Went to Cardiff to another situation. While there she took to secret drinking, lost her situation, and fell into the hands of a landshark, who brought her to Merthyr. They both got intoxicated, were locked up, but she, being a first offender, was handed over to me and taken to our Rescue Home in Cardiff.
3. Another woman aged 38, deserted by her husband three years ago. A man offered her whiskey, became intoxicated and was locked up. On being spoken to, she said, "I used to be pure once, but I am now as low as I can be." It is not always the fault of the fallen women. Man is to blame often, although he does not have to bear the brunt now.
4. One morning I went to meet the train from Swansea and saw a poor woman returning from prison. She said, "I little expected a kind friend to meet me coming from prison." We went to a café to have some breakfast, and she told me she never had a chance. "I go to prison, come out, go down again. There is nowhere for me to go but back to my old companions."

After questioning her, I found out that she used to sell fish. I bought a washing basket, half a hundredweight of bloaters, and set her on the way to help herself. She was so thankful that she continually came back telling me of her daily profits. She gave way to drink on one occasion since but is trying again to lead a better life. The whole family of this woman spend their time in prison. As one is coming out another is going in. But praise God He is able to save in apparently the most hopeless case. Kindness is the thing necessary to win these poor women, more than sermons.

Smiles will win them to God. There are choice gems in the heart if only we can reach them."

An appraisal of Sister Church's work at Pontypool

Here is Rev Watcyn Williams' appraisal of the work of Sister Church at Pontypool; [12]

> "I want to say a word about the Women's Branch. When thinking of it, I picture angels of mercy going about doing good. By now I have had the opportunity of seeing the practical side. How does it work? The more I look at it the more do I feel that we have lost tremendously by not starting it sooner. Had I to work a Centre now without the help of one of the Sisters, I should feel like a bird with one wing. Not only does the amount of the work demand such help but the nature of it more so. Here Sister Church has worked with a Christlike devotion, and many call her blessed. She carries the tenderness of Christ to the homes of the people and has created in many a longing to know more about the Saviour, and families are now regular attendants in the sanctuary, because through her, they saw some of the Saviour's glory, and the glory has drawn them over the line into the church. Her Christian winsomeness has captured young women who at first did things for her sake, but by today do them for His sake. Her hopefulness has laid hold of the despairing and made them start afresh. Homes are visited and helped and brightened by prayer and the Word. Young women are helped in their difficulties, encouraged in their efforts, and are quietly watched over, and guided by the eye of Christian love. The number that has been brought thus under Christian influence, which I could not touch, is legion. Whatever means may have attended the work of the Forward Movement here, no small part of it is due to the increasing labours of Sister Church; and yet how great is the work not done. Every day one is made to feel the awful extent of the wilderness: but God be praised, there are little vineyards coming to light. The work to some may look easy, and that is because they have never touched it. It is blood shedding work, and I thank God for godly women who are willing to bleed in the Master's service. Will you please pray for our good Sisters, and do what you can to help the Women's Branch in its loving ministry?"

A further comment on the work of Sister Church at Pontypool; [13]

> "How wonderfully God in His Providence opens the doors for His workers to enter with the message of salvation.
> Sister Church, who has worked heroically during the typhoid epidemic at Pontypool exposing herself to danger of infection, has had the joy of seeing many families attend the Forward Movement hall as a result of her relieving them in their suffering. 'I was sick and ye visited me.'

Statistics and Reports for the work of the Sisters of the People, 1903-1914

The Sisters of the People regularly submitted data on their work to the Superintendent of the Forward Movement, and they also reported on their work at conferences and committee meetings.

Here is an excerpt from the executive meeting of the Women's Branch as reported in 1909, where Sisters of the People gave a report;

> "To say we have eight Sisters of the People working in our most populous districts may convey little to most people, but when the monthly returns of these Sisters show that during the months of November, December, January (1908), over seven thousand homes were dealt with, visited, prayer offered and the scriptures read in about fourteen hundred homes, between two and three thousand were indifferent to their souls' welfare and attended no place of worship. One is astonished by the amount of work which is done through the agency of the Women's Branch. Our Committee has been singularly fortunate in its choice of workers and the harmony which exists in the work and the way in which God is blessing our efforts makes it evident that many remember the work at the Throne of Grace. Our Committee was mightily moved, and we experienced a little Heaven below as the Sisters, one after another, unfold a tale of Love triumphant over sin, sorrow, and shame, of broken hearts bound up, and sorrowing ones comforted. One Sister spoke from the fulness of her heart because she was receiving so much help from the Christian girls and women at the Centre, and it seemed that she was being carried along by the tide. Another Sister working in a poor slum district, told a tale of struggles against bitter odds, but a struggle in which the Man of Sorrows, The King of Kings was ever at her side." [14]

Similarly, a 'Glimpse at the Work of the Sisters of the People' from 1913 states;

> "This is a record of the work of two of the Sisters for the month of May (1913) who work in connection with the Forward Movement and taken from the Weekly Progress Sheets sent by them to the General Secretary of the Forward Movement."

Hours spent in visiting 296
Homes, workshops etc. visited 1125
Read and prayed in 294 homes of the homes visited
Sick visits 148, temporary relief given in several cases
Found 386 families who never attend a place of worship and induced 23 to attend, and several more promised.
Visited 15 houses of ill fame
Meetings held by the Sisters in and out of their districts 36
Pledges taken 6
Professed conversion 4
Average attendance in Sisters' meetings 40

(i) One of the Sisters reports that the woman who signed the pledge one week, during the last 12 months, had parted with everything, even the clothes off her back to get drink. She was in a terrible state when first seen, but now she is clothed and in her right mind.

(ii) The young woman who professed conversion was about 23 years of age. She has undergone a serious operation at the Infirmary. The Sister was there two or three times a week. In the midst of her trouble this poor young woman turned to the Lord and found peace.

(iii) A woman was induced to sign the pledge who had been leading an awful life and had been separated from her husband because of her drunken habits and evil life.

(iv) One of the women induced to attend the Hall had not been in a place of worship since she was a child. Now she has four children of her own.

(v) The Sister was sent to pray with a young girl who was thought to be dying. In her great stress and anxiety, she wanted someone to tell her about Jesus. The Sister told her the story of the Cross in a very simple way, she listened to it eagerly, and the tears streamed down her face.

> That night she found peace. Since then, she has recovered a little strength, and it is really beautiful to hear her tell others about the love of Jesus." [15]

Similarly glimpses of the work of the Sisters of the People appeared in the Treasury May 1913;

> "The young girl who came out for the Lord this week had for some time been leading a very wildlife, and I had almost despaired of her ever becoming any different. She seemed so very hard. At last I had the joy of seeing her coming out for Christ.
>
> The young woman who came out for Christ this week is in consumption, and when I first called to see her, she was very hard and very rebellious. She thought God was cruel to make her suffer so much. She would not listen to anything I said, neither would she let me pray with her. But after a few days she gave way, and told me her story, and a very sad one it was too. Now she has claimed Christ as her Saviour. To God be the praise."[16]

Come and see

E. G. Davies from North Wales visited Treborth Home on 30th December 1905 (just a month after it opened – much more about that later). During that visit, E. G. Davies went out visiting with Sister Alison Jones. He recalls;

> "After praying for guidance, our footsteps were directed to a little cottage, where we found a mother and daughter alone. The mother was a drunkard and was therefore a stumbling-block to her little daughter. The mother told us of her son who had gone to heaven. She was determined not to give up the drink as long as she lived, but after much pleading we sang the beautiful hymn 'Over the river faces I see.' Both mother and daughter came to the fountain for the blessed cleansing. The mother cried out, "Lord have mercy upon me: I have been a big sinner but have me now."
> The little daughter said, "Jesus save me now."

Both wished to meet the one who had gone before them in heaven, so in repentance they accepted Christ. We had the joy of seeing the mother at the cottage prayer meeting with a happy smile on her face.

'God moves in a mysterious way. His wonders to perform.' He makes big sinners into big saints. He put a new song in the mouth of a drunkard. There is wonder working power in the precious blood of the Lamb to cleanse even the vilest. Blessed be His Name." [17]

Chapter Three - Slum Stories from the Diary of Martha Jones, Sister of the People

(The Torch Feb/April/May 1910) [1]

This is a very simple account, but in its simplicity, it becomes incredibly profound. Please persevere to the end of the story.

Diary Entry One – Firewood Sally

There was a narrow street in Sea Beach. The houses were small, but six, seven often more human beings lived in each of them. In the first room on your left as you entered number 16 lives Miss Nelson, 'Firewood Merchant.' Her occupation consisted of cutting up old orange boxes, arranging them in bundles which she sold for a halfpenny each. The first time I visited her, Sally asked me in very graciously; at the same time she apologised for not being able to offer me a seat, as her only chair was in the pawn shop, "paying for the breakfast." It did not need very much knowledge to understand that Miss Nelson's breakfast did not consist of either tea or coffee!
"I have come!, I began, "to ask if you will come to our mother's meeting. It has just been started in connection with Moriah Chapel."
"Thank you for calling" replied Miss Nelson, "but I am not a mother, I am a single woman."
"Oh that doesn't matter in the least," I declared.
"We shall be very delighted to see you."
"I don't think I'll come to your meeting" she said.
"I have lived without religion for over 50 years, I can do without it till the end surely."
"Well!, I said, "you can come to the mother's meeting without being religious. I think you will enjoy it. We read stories and some of the young girls sing; come and see what sort of a meeting we have."
Miss Nelson shook her head.

"Religion," she said slowly.

"Is like that ere nasty influenza, it's a very catching thing – you never know how you catch it. There's Miss Bird the other side, she's been drinking every Saturday night as regular as the clock for 15 years an' more. She stays in bed all day Sunday to get sober an' then she's ready for work on Monday morning. But last Sunday week she heard that Deacon you've got in Moriah (the man with the big voice) shoutin' something in the open air an' Miss Bird ain't had no enjoyment of her drink since."

"Thank God." I said fervently.

"I knew you'd say that" said Miss Nelson, scornfully.

"That's the sort you are, grudgin' a bit o' henjoyment to poor folks; if you had your way there wouldn't be one public house in this town."

"Are you fond of a drink" I asked?

"No" answered Miss Nelson cheerfully. "I can live without the drink as well as anyone; of course sometimes I take more than is good for me. If I didn't drink I can tell you, I'd be living in a better street, but there, there, a short and merry one – that's my motto."

"There's a large tea party in our schoolroom next Tuesday night" I said.

"You shall have tea and cake and a concert for threepence."

"Well that's cheap enough, anyhow" said Miss Nelson.

"Here's my threepence and remember to call me Sally, not Miss Nelson. Sally suits my rags better."

Sally came to the tea party without having even washed her face, her clothes in rags and her feet peeping out of her boots. But having begun to come to Moriah, she came regularly every Tuesday afternoon to the mother's meeting, though her behaviour there was not good. She never tried to listen when the chapters were being read, or when prayers were being offered. One afternoon one of the sisters present gave an account of the missionary work in India and she entreated the mothers, if they could not give money towards the work to give their prayers.

The following Tuesday, Sally appeared with a basket full of firewood.

"I can't pray for them in India," she told everyone

"I don't believe in prayer, but if a bit 'll help 'em, they're heartily welcome to these bundles."

Every woman in the meeting suddenly had the desire to possess one of these bundles, so we raised the price of firewood and instead of receiving a halfpenny a bundle, we sold the dozen for two shillings, much to Sally's surprise. The following Tuesday, Sally's place was empty. She had, however, sent a message by her neighbour for me.

"Tell Sister Jones as I can't come any more to them meetings, an' she's not to worry about me, for I've a good bit of work an' no time at present for goin' to meetings."

I called many times to see her, but always found the door locked against me. I had a shrewd suspicion that Sally was not away from home, but for some reason best known to herself, she did not wish to see me or to encourage my visits. But I was just as determined as she: and one very wet afternoon, when the rain was pouring incessantly, I resolved to try again to storm the citadel.

Sally was caught unawares standing by her doorstep, and she could not do less than ask me into the room.

"I was bound to see you," I said.

"For we miss you from mother's meeting. Come on Sally, what has gone wrong?"

For a few moments I could get no reply.

"Oh Sister Jones," she cried.

"You've done a very bad piece of work. That old religious influenza is on me. But mind you" she added resolutely.

"I am taking good medicine to cure it. I get drunk every day regularly. I don't get time to be religious."

I scarcely knew how to answer her, and my silence became so long that Sally broke in impatiently.

"You are worth nothing as a pedlar" she said contemptuously.

"If I told one of 'em that I felt I wanted a bit of cloth very bad, but that I didn't mean to buy today, I'd be obliged to take the cloth. I'd never get rid of the pedlar if I didn't, but you good folks, you aren't half so anxious to get people to believe in your God. 'You'd better come to Jesus Christ, you say, but you MAKE 'em come to Him.'

Her words burnt me like fire, I felt that they were true. Very humbly I tried to speak a word for Jesus, tried to tell this poor sin tossed person of the life eternal which He promised to a sinner.

"I don't care a pin's head for eternal life,' Sally said mutinously.

"I don't know in the world what you are talking about."

"Well," I asked. "How do you know that you want religion?"

"There's some old pain bothering me," she said.

"Somethin' sounding in my ears all the time, Come to Jesus, Come to Jesus and I don't want to Come to Jesus, there's nothing about me."

"No," I interrupted, he is worth coming to. Let me tell you how tender, how loving, how gentle he is.

"Don't bother about me," Sally cried.

"My folk always live long, but there's a poor young woman upstairs dyin' as quick as she can of consumption. You'd better go to see her. If she got a bit of religion, maybe 'twould help her a bit."

"I'll come with you now," I said.

Diary Entry Two – My Lady of Tantrums

I prepared to follow Sally upstairs to visit the sick woman, when I suddenly happened to glance at my companion and I noticed to my delight that Sally looked much cleaner than on those occasions when she condescended to visit our mother's meeting. But if the mistress of the house was cleaner, the poor room which constituted her home seemed barer and emptier than ever. I could see no trace even of a bed.

"Sally," I asked sympathetically. "Are times very bad."

"No indeed ma'am," she replied sturdily. "Things are better than usual with me – this little woman upstairs has a rich aunt, and she pays me for looking after Mrs Hunt."

"Where do you sleep now," I enquired?

"Oh," Sally answered shortly, "I have sold the old bed and now I'm like the grand folks, I sleeps in a bedroom; we'd better go and see Mrs Hunt now."

I followed her up the narrow staircase to a comfortably furnished little room. A bright fire was burning in the grate, and on a clean, new bed, a young woman was lying, with death's cold fingers traced on her white face.

"Where have you been"? she called angrily, turning to Sally.

"I'll be sure to tell my aunt what sort of a nurse you are."

"This woman," she continued looking at me and pointing with a trembling finger to Sally. "This creature takes payment from my dear aunt for nursing me and instead of doing so, she leaves me alone for hours at a time. She's an old thief."

A fit of coughing stopped the flow of her eloquence and Sally very gently lifted her up and helped her. When it was over, the sick girl (for she was little more) was too exhausted to speak and I went home marvelling at the sweet patience of Firewood Sally.

I often called to see Mrs Hunt, though I must confess that visiting her was far from being a pleasure. It was impossible to please her – everyone, so she declared, with the exception of her rich aunt, was very disagreeable to her. Her treatment of Sally pained me very much. Sally had not had much experience in nursing, but she waited on her peevish, discontented patient with quite exemplary patience and the only thanks, vouchsafed to her was a storm of abuse.

"She is an old thief. It's in prison she ought to be. She's a drunken creature. She is never sober."

These were the terms in which Mrs Hunt described Sally to me: and I often wondered how Sally bore those rebuffs so meekly. The only person of whom Mrs Hunt spoke well was the rich aunt and she loved to boast of her riches.

"How is it," I asked one day, "that your aunt never comes to see you?"

"Oh," Mrs Hunt replied, "It hurts her to see me so poor: she comes occasionally upstairs, but never comes into my room, she's that sensitive: she throws a parcel through the door and away she goes. She never shows herself."

"What is there in the parcels," I asked.

"Oh money," she replied.

"But it's precious little I get; that old Sally steals the most of it."

There was very little evidence of money to be seen in the room. There was a comfortable fire to be sure, a clean bed, but very little else. It was very difficult to get Mrs Hunt willing to listen to a word about the great world beyond. In spite of the fact that every breath cost her a tremendous effort, and though she became weaker day-by-day, she yet believed that she was regaining her strength. One day, I noticed that she was far weaker than I had ever seen her, and if that were possible, she was more peevish than usual. Everything was wrong. I cope with her as best I could; and then at last asked her if she would like me to read a portion of God's Word.

"t's as you like, you'll do," she answered sarcastically.

"It don't matter if I'm willing or not, nobody thinks of me."

I bit my lips and read a few of the sweet consoling words of John 14, when suddenly Mrs Hunt interrupted me.

"Your horrid Welsh accent hurts me," she said petulantly.

I had borne a great deal that afternoon and this was the last straw.

"I have put up with your bad temper for a long time," I said severely.

"Goodbye." I opened the door and found Sally standing outside.

"You aren't leaving her," she cried sadly.
"Indeed I am." I replied hotly. "I have no time to stay here to be insulted by Mrs Hunt."
"She is very ill, nearly dying," said Sally softly.
"And she doesn't know Jesus poor thing."
"Do you know him Sally?" I asked in surprise.
"A little bit," replied Sally.

Data Entry Three – "One of the Best"

"What shall we do for Mrs Hunt," Sally asked me one day.
"She dying,' as she can, and she won't listen to no one."
"I can do no more for her," I replied.
"I have tried to speak to her of the tenderness of Jesus and she laughs sarcastically. I tell her of the judgement that is surely coming, and she gets into a frenzy of passion and declares that she has never done any harm to anyone. I really have done my best for her."
"I believe you have," said Sally. "But what can we do.?" "She is dying and I don't want her to die like that."
Our conversation is interrupted by the entrance of a neighbour, who told Sally that Mrs Hunt was trying to call her. I followed Sally upstairs and stood for a moment outside the door. To my horror, I saw Mrs Hunt lay hold to Sally's hair, pulling it fiercely. She was too weak to do much harm, but the expression on her face was diabolic. I went home feeling miserable and depressed. Mrs Hunt was a wicked woman, but she had an immortal soul. Would God hold me responsible if she were lost? My conscience pricked me. Had I any right to be feeling so angry with her? She had offended me, and I had run away from her in anger. God taught me a deep lesson that day. I could not rest in my comfortable little room. Some power greater than myself made me put my coat on and go down once again to the house. I met very few and quietly I mounted the uneven stairs and stood outside the door to Mrs Hunt's room. Ah! God had spoken to me in no uncertain voice! I had allowed my anger to control my actions. I had left a poor, human soul to battle as best it might against the briars and thorns of sin, but the Good Shepherd had not forgotten the lost sheep! The door was not quite closed and I could hear voices in the room, so I stepped in very quietly and sat on a chair without disturbing anyone. It was a wonderful revelation! On her knees by the bedside was Sally doing her best to lead Mrs Hunt to the Saviour of the world.

"Try to say, Jesus take me, He'll take you at once," said Sally.

"And there's a fine one He is – He never keeps tellin' you of old sins, what He says to you is 'my little child, you lie quiet in my arms, I'll take care of you always.'

"Just you try Him Mrs Hunt dear."

In a very weak voice Mrs Hunt replied, "Oh, I'm too bad, I used to think I was pretty good, but I know now that I am a great sinner. Jesus will never take me."

"Look here," said Sally.

"Have you ever been drunk?"

"No," answered Mrs Hunt. "I've always been a respectable women, always."

"Well," said Sally, "I've been drinking for years and yet Jesus took me so He's sure to take you."

"Oh I am a very great sinner," said Mrs Hunt. I'm afraid of God.

"You must do as I did," said Sally.

"I said to God – Oh Lord don't look at me, but look at the Blood of Jesus, which is flowing like a river over my bad heart, and that's just what He did. He didn't look at my sin, the Blood of Jesus had covered 'em."

"There's a verse somewhere," said Mrs Hunt, "that says that God is a Shepherd. I remember hearing it years ago. I'd love to hear it again."

I thought the time had come for me to make my presence known, and although my eyes were wet with tears, I read to the two wondering women, the sweet, soothing words of the 23rd Psalm. Mrs Hunt could not say much, but as I was leaving the room, she whispered, "Go to my aunt and ask her to be very kind to Sally, thank her for all her kindness, I should have died long ago if it hadn't been for the money which she sent."

"Would you like to see your aunt," I asked.

"Very much," the sick woman replied.

"But she'll have to hurry, I'm going fast."

"But you're a holding on to the Good Shepherd?"

"Yes," she answered softly. "Sally's pushed me close to Him and He is holding me."

Diary Entry Four – "In as much …"

Very early the next morning I went to the door of Mrs Perkins. The lady herself opened the door.

"I have come from your niece," I began, "she is very ill."

"Tell her I never give to beggars. I washed my hands of her years ago. She and her tantrums don't suit me."

"But," I retorted, "she's dying – if you don't come very quickly she'll be gone and she wanted to see you to thank you for your kindness to her."

It struck me that Mrs Perkins seemed surprised, but I attached little meaning just then to her expression.

"You will not be long will you," I added.

"I have made a rule," said Mrs Perkins unimpressively, "never to miss my meals, you always suffer when you do. As soon as I've eaten my breakfast I'll come along with you Sister Jones to see my poor niece. I'm of a forgiving nature."

It tried my patience terribly to see Mrs Perkins sitting calmly and comfortably by her table, sipping tea and eating toast as leisurely as if death would wait for our convenience. But at last she finished, carried the soiled china into the scullery, and, with a smile, put on her bonnet and coat. When we reached the house we discovered that Mrs Hunt had just passed away, and Mrs Perkins was very reluctant even to enter the house.

"Take no responsibility," she adjured, "I'm only a poor widow and it's my duty to see to myself. I've no money to waste, and now she's dead, the parish can bury her. I pays my rates regular."

"Your niece particularly asked you to be kind to Sally," I said sternly. "Of course, I don't know what arrangements you have made."

"Arrangements," she echoed, "what are you talking about, I've made no arrangements with Sally or anyone else."

"But you've been here asking for your niece," I said.

"Never," she returned, "I've never put my foot in this dirty street until today. I'd like you to understand that I'm a very respectable woman Sister Jones and though I says it as shouldn't, I've a nice little sum in the bank that no one can touch but me."

I said no more, but my mind was busy pondering!

"My poor niece's bed looks pretty new," Mrs Perkins said presently, running her eyes appraisingly over the furniture of the room.

"I'm the next of kin and I've no use for this bed, so let Sally what's her name have everything that's in this room. That'll pay her handsome for tending my poor niece."

And having delivered herself of this oration, Mrs Perkins disappeared and I have not seen her since.

Sometime after Mrs Hunt's burial, I went to visit Sally. The poor room looked more comfortable and homely than I had ever seen it. Suddenly Sally turned to me.

"Sister Jones," she asked with some confusion.

"Is it wrong to tell lies if you don't get nothing through them."

"Yes, a lie is always wrong," I replied.

"Well, well, there's no hope for me then," said Sally sadly.

"God is ready to forgive if we only repent and resolve to tell the truth henceforth. So, now if you are really sorry, and ask for forgiveness, all will be well." "The blood of Jesus Christ, His Son cleanseth us from all sin," said Sally. "There's fine He is to die for me! I can never thank him enough."

"Sally," I asked, "how did you find Jesus?"

"Twas He found me indeed Sister." said Sally. "I didn't want to be as Christian, an' I did my best against that religious influenza, as I know Sister like this it was. I saw that Mrs Hunt – poor thing – was dying, and it's an awful thing to die. I saw a good old woman die once and I've never forgotten how happy she was. I said then, as I was bound to get religion before I died, but I didn't want none to live by. I could live without Jesus first rate, but I was afraid to die without Him. And when I saw Mrs Hunt – poor thing – I thought I was bound to get a bit of religion for her; that's why I wanted to go to see her, it was very slow she was taking religion, but I used to do best I could, talking to her about Jesus. I didn't know much about Him, but I was trying to remember everything I'd ever heard about Him and I used to repeat those things over and over to Mrs Hunt. And one day as I was chopping the wood, something said to me quite plainly, 'Sally, you are the Lord's child'."

"No indeed I'm not," said I back again.

"It's an old Pagan I am."

"You are the Lord's daughter," said the voice again.

"All nonsense," said I, and then I thought I heard some voice asking me, 'Sally do you love Me?'

"Yes indeed I do, Lord Jesus," said I.

"Do you try to get others to love me?"

"Yes indeed," said I. "I'd like just to see all the street loving Jesus."

"Do you want to give yourself to the Son of God," asked the voice?

"Of course I do if He can do anything with me. And then I thought I heard him saying.

"You are the Lord's servant."

"Oh but," said I, "I've got sins, such a heap I can't count 'em." What'll I do with them?" And thought that was the end of everything. But just then I saw the Cross you've been talking about. Jesus was hanging on it and I saw that my sins were hanging there too. Oh I felt so happy. But by and by I remembered about drink. I've been a terror for my glass. And what do you think Jesus said?

"Sally you just throw your temptations on Me: let me fight instead of you. And that's what I did. I threw all the work on Jesus. I don't know how He and the devil have done things, but every time I get tempted to drink I say to him, 'leave me alone I have nothing to do with you. Jesus is fighting my battles and then I don't see him for a bit. He's too frightened of Jesus I expect. And after Jesus had done such a lot for me I thought I'd ask Him a favour to save poor Mrs Hunt, and He did I'm sure of that."

"Sally," I said quietly.

"You know Jesus better than I do. Tell me how much Mrs Perkins used to pay you for nursing Mrs Hunt."

Sally reddened but did not say one word.

"Ah, I understand now," I said with a laugh.

"Mrs Perkins never paid you a farthing."

"No," Sally replied.

"What about those parcels of pennies Mrs Hunt used to say her aunt threw into the room?"

"Well if you must know," said Sally.

"I gave them. She was very poor, and very proud, poor little thing and I knew she'd break her heart if she was taken to the workhouse. She gave me a letter to post to her aunt one day, and she was expecting an answer every day. It was pitiful to see her, so as I had a few coppers by me I packed 'em up and threw them into the room, and pretending to find them when I came a bit later. Mrs Hunt thought her aunt couldn't stand to see how poor she was.

"You gave her your bed too," I said.

"I knew Mrs Hunt wouldn't want it for long."

"Where did you sleep meanwhile," I asked?

"Oh, I did alright." "Sometimes I slept on the floor, sometimes by Mrs Hunt's side.

Do you know Sister Jones, I was earning money without any trouble, while Mrs Hunt was ill. The pennies were coming in one after the other without any stop. God was looking after us you see.

So, Firewood Sally became a missionary in her own street. Her zeal for Jesus Christ was very lovely. She would hand her clothes to the different women in the street and if Sally was herself absent from the services, you might be very sure that her clothes were there adorning one or other of the women.

It would be impossible to estimate the effect of Sally's life and conduct in her street.

Chapter Four – Treborth Preventative Home

John Pugh was very concerned about the friendless girls; especially the wild, undisciplined girl from a poor home, whose schooling was over, but who had not settled into any suitable job. Similarly, he was concerned for the despised prostitutes roaming the streets, exploited by evil men, spurned by the morally decent, and 'passed by on the other side' by the churches.

John Pugh had a vision for a home for friendless girls and fallen women and the Women's Branch of the Forward Movement understood the need and took on the work of realising the vision. It was the 1904-05 revival that brought middle class church women face to face with a new challenge – the unusual presence of converted prostitutes in their church congregations.

Mrs Richard Davies of Treborth Hall, Bangor, North Wales, wife of the non-conformist politician, made a very generous donation towards the setting up of a Preventative Home.

In 1905 it is recorded;

> "At the Glamorgan Presbytery meeting at Tonypandy, October 19th, the recommendation of the Building Committee was unanimously adopted viz. That we buy No. 2 and No. 4 Corporation Road, Grangetown, Cardiff, for the establishment of the first Preventative Home. As is well known, we have been enabled to purchase one of these houses through the generosity of Mrs Davies, Treborth, Bangor, and we hope to open the home on Thursday 30th November." [1]

And thus in gratitude to Mrs Richard Davies, the home was given the name 'Treborth Preventative Home' and it was opened on 30th November 1905.

Some detail on the opening ceremony for the Treborth Preventative Home, 2–4 Corporation Road, Grangetown, Cardiff are recorded as follows;

> "The opening of Treborth Home on Thursday November 30th was, despite the inclemency of the weather, a most pleasant and inspiring function.

Mrs John Pugh (President) to whom Mrs Walter Lloyd presented the key to the premises, in declaring the home open, expressed her appreciation of the honour of taking such a part in a function of such momentous issue in the history of our Denomination. After, the friends assembled entered the house. The dedication service was held in the Board Room, and a striking address was delivered by Rev. Gwilym Jones of Penarth. After the home had been inspected and all had expressed their admiration of its homelike and comfortable appearance, tea was served by the Grangetown ladies and was followed by a lively and helpful Conference of Women's work generally and the ordering and supporting of the Home." [2]

In the report from the Women's Branch in the Torch in February 1906, it states;

"Treborth Home has been the means already of not merely keeping from evil, but of leading souls to the Saviour. Why! They have had Pentecostal showers there, and that within a month of it's establishment" [2a]

What an amazing encouragement and endorsement of all that they sought to do at the Home.

Sister Lloyd, who was the first matron at Treborth Preventative Home gave an interesting insight into one aspect of the work, as recorded in 1907; Sister Jones and Sister Watkins also resided at the Home.

"Endurance and daring – patience and boldness – these are the weapons which, with God's help, we are going to use in our fight against sin and impurity, in our endeavours to lift their victims and restore them.
Recently I had to attend a Police court in the Rhondda Valley for the purpose of getting the magistrates to allow me to take a young girl, convicted of theft, to the Home, in order to save her from a life of sin. It was a great joy for me, when in the witness box, to be able to speak of the good work which our Home, purchased by a dear benefactress, and supported by the Calvinistic Methodists and other friends, was doing. "This is, indeed, practical Christianity," remarked one of the magistrates. A morning spent in the Police court convinces one of the need for women workers and for Preventative Homes, because, I grieve to say it, it is so

> often necessary to remove the young from the baneful influence of their mothers and their homes. This is what one sees there – a little child of eight, convicted of stealing salt-cellars, at the instigation of her mother; a child of eleven, on several charges of robbery, the mother being a good for nothing. Juvenile criminality is one of the awful problems which the magistrates in Wales have to face – and that in the majority of cases because there is no home influence, because the parents cannot or will not perform their obligation.
>
> Who will take the light into these sin-darkened homes? Who will teach our mothers to teach their little ones to follow only the right? How great is the need for consecrated women workers in the populous districts of South Wales, only those who live there can realise." [3]

The Treborth Preventative Home situated at 2 – 4 Corporation Road, Grangetown, Cardiff was soon to be replaced by bigger premises that could extend the work to Rescue as well as preventative. The new premises were at 379 Cowbridge Road East, Canton, Cardiff.

Miss Frances Jefferies, who replaced Sister Lloyd as matron at Treborth Home (Sister Lloyd returning to her duties as Sister of the People at Saltmead) writes in 1908 the final report for Treborth Home as follows;

> "I have much pleasure in giving this month the Matron's Report of the work attempted at Treborth Home. We have much cause to rejoice over the lives saved through the Home, and much reason to mourn for the devastation wrought by the evil one on the lives of some of our young girls, who, though every chance was given them to start afresh, have been unable to free themselves from the fetters of sin.
>
> From the opening of the Treborth Home, December 1905 to April 1908, 61 cases in all have been admitted. Of these 22 girls have been sent to service; 17 sent to other homes; 15 restored to friends, 2 are now in residence, and 5 left of their own accord. Three of our service girls have kept their places 12 months, and three have been just over six months. These figures may convey little to the mind as one scans this page, but to those who have the girls' welfare at heart they mean a great deal. Looking back over our 'case book' each name brings before us some particular nature to form or mould as He sees best. Many have been the prayers offered for each girl, and many the offers of help made and

repeated. Often we have been downcast, and then God has stepped in, taken the helm of the young lives, and piloted them safe through the perils we dreaded for them. Here is a peep at our home life:-

Half past six finds the household astir. Housework occupies the earlier hours with an interval at 8.30 for breakfast, which is followed by prayers. The housework finished, and every room having been made spick and span, the sewing is brought out.

Dinner is served at 1.30, tea at 5, and supper at 8.30. At 9 o'clock, weary but happy, our girls retire, thankful for the shelter and protection afforded by our Home.

We have had some very happy times and helpful around our Family Altar morning and evening, and the girls are encouraged to ask questions and take part in prayers. They often write and speak of it when away in service. One girl writes: "I often think of you all at night, and sometimes I long to be with you, but I am in spirit."

Another writes, "I had known no home until I came to Treborth."

Another writes, "I thank God for sending me to you."

A real home is the ideal aimed at, and not a 'barrack sort of existence.'

It is a great joy to know that our girls are doing well in service.

One mistress writes, "M.J. is a splendid girl, and I am so thankful to you for sending her."

Another writes, "A P is a treasure. I would not lose her for anything."

Another writes, "E is a really good girl, far better than my older maid, and so trustworthy."

Another writes, "L is a hardworking, painstaking, and trustworthy girl and is well worth her money."

Now let me take you to an imaginary visit to our kitchen, and you see there seated around the table a family of eight girls, two of these having been newly admitted. The elder of the two can scarcely sit at the table properly, and I really think that knives and forks are foreign to her. This poor girl comes from a bad home, and her parents wished her to go on the streets to support them. Another little mite was almost too frightened to look up, but now she is the brightest of our family. Another girl's parents had no control over her and could do simply nothing with her. We took her in but felt like giving up two or three times. Now through His wonderful power, she has conquered, and is striving to fight under His banner.

My time is drawing to a close. Eighteen months have passed away and my one aim has been that others may know Him, and I have tried to fulfil my mission. May I ask that the new Home and inmates be upheld in prayer, and especially those who are in authority may be endowed with wisdom and power from on high. I sign myself for the last time, Frances Jefferies, Matron of Treborth Home. [4]

Thus the Treborth Preventative Home at 2 – 4 Corporation Road, Grangetown, Cardiff closed. It was very limited in its capacity - being two four bedroomed terraced houses. It was only able to carry on preventative work, i.e. preventing young girls from falling into gross sin. However, the vision was for a bigger premises, so that the work could be extended to include a rescue work, i.e. rescue young girls who had fallen.

In 1907, Mrs S M Saunders, secretary of the Women's Branch writes;

"In addition to the preventative work, we are hoping to have the honour and privilege of doing rescue work. He, who left us an example that we should follow His steps, distinctly told us that His business in life was "to seek and to save that which was lost". The title which He best loved was "Friend of publicans and sinners" I thank Him for letting a women who was a sinner wash His feet with her tears and for uttering those words of heavenly love, "Thy sins are forgiven, go in peace" There are still women in this city waiting to wash His feet with their tears, waiting to hear His voice telling them, "Thy sins are forgiven go in peace" There are close behind us, women living in sin, while around them stand the mocking multitude with their hideous morality – ready to stone them; and they are waiting to hear a voice, gentle, yet authoritative, saying to them "Neither do I condemn thee; go and sin no more" [4a]

Thus, the work moved to a fine four-storied house, standing in its own grounds off Cowbridge Road, Canton, Cardiff. The house when purchased was called Kingswood, so the name of the new home became Kingswood Treborth Rescue and Preventative Home, and the story continues in the next chapter.

Chapter Five – Kingswood – Treborth Rescue and Preventative Home

Courtesy of the Presbyterian Church of Wales, Treasury Magazine Aug 1908
The Rescue Home, Cardiff

Here are excerpts from the account of the opening of Kingswood Treborth Home, which appeared in the newspaper on 8th May 1908;

> "Mrs Davies of Plas Dinam on arriving at Kingswood was heartily welcomed by a large company. Mrs Davies having been presented with a gold key by the architect opened the new home amidst applause, and she expressed the hope that it would be the means of doing excellent work in Cardiff, where girls were subjected to many temptations.
> Rev. J. Williamson, President of the Cardiff and District Free Churches Council said such work as was carried out through the agency of Rescue and Preventative homes did much to vindicate Christianity in the sight of the world.

> Mrs Walter Lloyd, (Aberdare) said wild birds, animals etc. were protected. There was equal need for the protection of young girls, especially in large centres of population.
> The objects of the home are 'to befriend friendless girls, to save fallen women, to succour neglected children, and to care for the sick and dying among the lapsed masses of our great towns." [5]

Thus, the Kingswood Treborth Rescue and Preventative Home was opened on the 7th of May 1908. Rev. George Howe (minister at Saltmead) was Superintendent of the Home for the first year and Mrs Howe was the first Matron, again for the first year. Their co-workers were Sister Elise Williams and Sister Janet Roberts (the outdoor and police court visitor).

The first year at Kingswood-Treborth Home

An account of the work at the Home during the first year written by Rev. George Howe, Superintendent follows;

> "Here is a record of the work during the first year, called from the carefully typed reports that are submitted each month to the Committee. Bare figures are all that can be supplied. Behind them lie hard work, great sacrifice, loving patience, many tears and prayers – a blessed offering that is delightful to the Redeemer's heart.
>
> 53 friendless, fallen women have found rest, good counsel and temporary aid in the shelter.
> 14 poor betrayed women and girls have found their way back to virtue, industry and God, having passed through the Home to suitable situations.
> 12 girls and women have been restored to their friends, as follows – 7 girls to their parents, 2 to their relatives and 3 wives to their husbands and families, 6 young women deceived by heartless wretches under the promise of marriage, have been cared for with their babies, and are now with friends, or in situations. Suitable arrangements having been made for the babies, so that the mothers might be free to earn their own living and support their children. Whenever possible, the father of the child is

traced, and his wrong-doing brought home to him – and he is made to comply with certain conditions that meet the demands of justice.

There are at present in the Home 26 -women and girls and one baby, making the grand total 126 – women, girls and babies sheltered, rescued and many of them saved during the year.

The women and girls come to the Home in all conditions, needing particular advice, treatment and help. They come friendless, mental, physical and moral wrecks: drunken, unclean and practically naked. Others come well dressed, sick and tired of their manner of living. Destitute girls, on the point of falling into sin, have and are being protected and assisted.

Young women, while free from the committal of the deeper and darker sins of impurity, when brought up surrounded by scenes of vice, have evil thoughts flooding their minds. Frequently, too, their conception of right and wrong is very mixed – they cannot distinguish truth from falsehood. An awful condition of disposition and temper manifest themselves in some, requiring a strong controlling oversight.

Again, the intellectual capacity of the younger girls leaves much to be desired. These wayward girls from such impure environments – for here is one, reported to be born drunk, several brought to the Home uncontrollable, and whose parents have no authority over them whatsoever – all of them require special training, long patience and a true mother's love and management.

Women long lost and fallen into the depths, one having been in prison over 60 times, another over 120 times, women having become creatures debased below the level of the brutes. Lewd of gesture, foul of language and life, are becoming respectable, and having a new start in life by earning their own living and giving satisfaction to their employers.

During the period that the inmates are in the Home suitable and useful employment is daily arranged for each one, such as house cleaning, cooking, washing, ironing, mending etc. Every young woman and girl admitted has therefore, an opportunity of becoming proficient in domestic duties. There are about 16 engaged in the Laundry, which is being well patronised. Reasonable time is allowed for recreation after meals, also in the evening after work. Their happy laughter, the cheerfulness, the contentment of those anxious to lead a better life. The devotion of morning and evening family worship, and the fact that the girls who are in service spend their evenings out at the Home, shows that 'Kingswood-Treborth' is not a formal institution, but a Home of help and love. All are trained to be obedient, to cultivate habits of industry, truthfulness, honesty, punctuality, and temperance in all things; to avoid waste, which leads to want; to show kindness one to another, and above all – each one in personal interviews, and in the religious services is urged to seek the way to salvation, through repentance and faith in our Lord Jesus Christ." [6]

Testimonies from the early years

And as recorded in 'The Torch,' October 1910, here are some individual testimonies from the early years of Kingswood – Treborth Rescue and Preventative Home;

> B. – a girl who came to the Home 16 months ago, aged 16. She was ruined when only 11 years old. During her stay at the Home she had to be sent twice to the Lock Word. Having been restored in body and mind, and having been redeemed in spirit, she has gone to service with Mrs J. at E. and is giving evidence of a changed life and heart.

> J. aged 22. Betrayed and came to the Home six months ago, blighted in character and broken in spirit. The loving care she received and the grace of the Saviour have restored this young woman to hope, health, and character. She is happy and gives satisfaction in the situation which has been found for her with Mrs Evans.

F. aged 20. Came to the Home six months ago from the Police Court. Mother and sister all prostitutes. When she came to us she was covered in scars and bruises from ill treatment. Dull and helpless, she had no idea about house duties, nor even could she keep herself clean. After six months a new light came into her mind and shone in her countenance – the evidence of the soul's awakening to the reality of the Saviour's love. She has developed into a thoughtful girl, and has gone to service to Mrs M." [7]

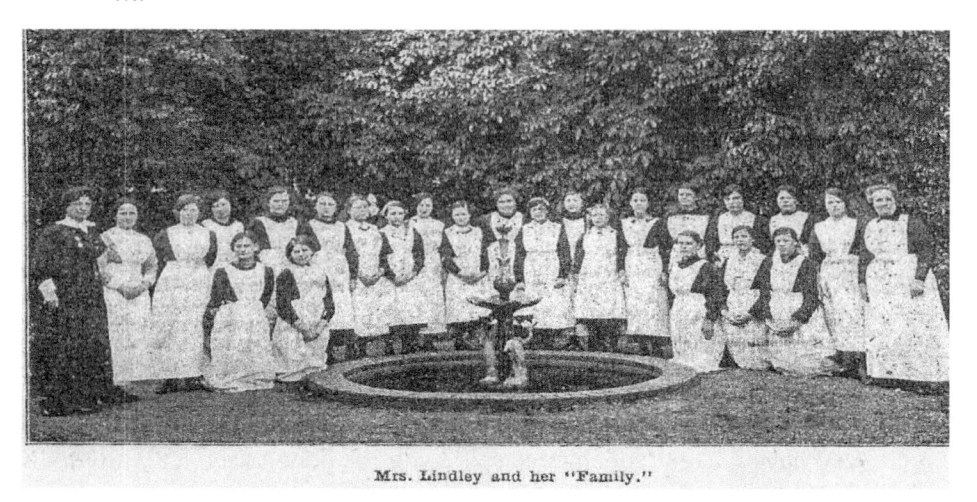

Mrs. Lindley and her "Family."

Courtesy of the Presbyterian Church of Wales, Treasury magazine Sept 1915

The wider work of the Home

The Sisters of the People went out from the Rescue and Preventative Home to visit the Union Workhouse, attend the police courts, the police cells, and prison gates, thus trying to get in touch with the girls who most needed help – a kind word, a helping hand outstretched to the despairing. They also gave out invitation cards, as indicated below.

The Sisters of the People also went out from the Home to hold 'midnight meetings' in a room in areas where prostitutes were known to be. A cup of tea was provided, then a hymn was sung, followed by a very short gospel message, and then time to talk. Some prostitutes only came in for a warm and a cup of tea, but some stayed longer. As the girls passed out of the room, a card was presented to each one, with the following;

If any young woman or girl wants a friend, help or advice, call or write

Kingswood Treborth, 379 Cowbridge Road, Canton, Cardiff.

These were distributed at the midnight meetings, in houses of ill fame, in the streets, or to any poor girl who looked like she needed help.

This is a conversation between one of the Sisters of the People and an attendee at a midnight meeting in 1908:

> "You can do nothing for me, don't you see that I am that creature which they call a fallen woman – an unfortunate? There is nothing for me but to make the best of life down here, for there will never be any other possible."
>
> "Jesus asked me," replied the Sister, "to lend Him my hands, my arms, my voice, and to go down and say to you, 'I will help you to rise;' you can't see Him, though He is close by, but it is He who is speaking to you, it is His Hand that is touching you, for before I came here I told Him that I was only willing to come here on condition that He used my body and touched my hand and spoke with my voice. You cannot refuse Him."
>
> And the tears came into her bleary eyes.
>
> "I thought it sounded better than your voice would," she said dreamily. "Tell me was it you who wanted to save me, or He who wanted you to save me."
>
> "Oh it was He who told me to come," the Sister answered. "Why I should have been too frightened to try, lest I should fail, but when He said, 'I will use your arms and hands and voice,' I knew that failure was impossible."
>
> "I wonder why He cares so much," the woman asked. "Look at me – a drunken sot, that's what I am, and I might have been a respectable woman, instead of that I am, a drunken, fallen woman, my own sister wouldn't own me if we met on the street; and yet He cares; I don't understand it."
>
> "No one can," said the Sister. "It is too wonderful, but you see, you and I cost Him a great deal – He bore the cross for us, so we have become too precious to be lost."
>
> "Did He tell you to say, 'you and I'?" was the next question.
>
> "Certainly, isn't He using my voice?"
>
> "Oh I wish He didn't care so much; I wish He wasn't so tender, it's that that kills," she said in anguish.

"He has loved you so long, He has taken such pains, such trouble to save you, I didn't want to come here tonight, it has meant a lot of worry, but He told me to come for some special purpose. He wanted to have the loan of me to save you. Will you disappoint Him?"

"I can't. I can't. Oh I could resist you very well, I could turn a deaf ear to your pleading, but He is different, I believe I love Him already; but I am too weak to move."

"Then stay still and let Him lift you; don't you remember that 'He gathers the lambs with His arms, and carries them in his bosom,' that's the kind of Saviour He is."

"I must come but not tonight."

"You will let Him be disappointed, grieved after all His trouble."

"I can't do that." She fell on her knees. "Lord Jesus, pull me away; I want to come, and I don't want to come; pull me, Lord Jesus Christ."

Do you think the prayer will be unanswered? No, a thousand times 'No,' sooner or later His Word will return to Him, and it will not be void.[8]

These midnight meetings, Oh the sorrow of them, the horrible waste; these bright young lives tainted and marred by sin! And yet there are beautiful trophies of grace. One girl, once a drunken profligate, but the Son of God touched her, she heard His voice saying to her, "Neither do I condemn thee: go, and sin no more."

There was power in His voice, and she claimed victory through His Blood. And the battle was won; she is earning a respectable livelihood now, and whenever she can get away she comes to the midnight meeting to help her old companions to place their guilt 'under the Blood.'

Highlights and Lowlights at the Home

Ceridwen Peris, who was on the Home Committee, visited the Home in summer 1915 for a garden fete arranged by the Matron to enlarge the funds. Over 250 friends attended. A short but interesting entertainment was given by the girls. The Matron had taken great pains to train the girls. The singing comprised of English part songs, Welsh melodies, and also recitations in English and Welsh. Four marquees had been put up, under whose shade tea and sweets and fruit were served; all the cakes, jellies, lemonades etc. being made by the girls in the Home. It was understood that the day proved a financial success.

Ceridwen Peris commented that, " I have great pleasure in testifying to the high tone of the Home. It is really a school for useful domestic work and high moral training. The girls are happy, and a general ambition to excel pervades all. Mrs Lindley, the Matron, is held in high esteem by the girls, and their attachment to the Home is quite evident. When they leave for situations, they are glad to visit Home – most of them have no other home, and they are always welcomed by Mrs Lindley and Sister Pierce, her faithful helper. They are advised as to the best way to spend their wages etc. and they confide and freely tell their difficulties. Eventually the girls may become wives and mothers, and it is hoped that in their own homes they will emulate all they have learned at Kingswood-Treborth Home." [8a]

Another highlight for the Home was recorded in 1938;

> "How valuable is the Home's assistance in helping girls to a suitable place in life is shown by a recent instance whereby one of the girls passed the entrance exam for the Civil Service and is at the present moment a typist at Whitehall. He who cares for the 'ones' must rejoice that this lamb that was sheltered by the Home has been kept and equipped for larger opportunities." [9]

There were, however, a number of lowlights for the Home. As recorded in the newspaper in October 1925;

> "A young girl's allegations of cruelty against Kingswood-Treborth Home, Cardiff were investigated at Newport Police Court where A.A. of Liswerry, Newport was brought up on remand for a breach of court order. At a previous court it was stated that she had been bound over on condition that she entered Kingswood-Treborth Home, Cardiff, but she subsequently absconded from the Home. She made allegations against the conduct of the Home. Frances Jeffries, the Matron of the Home in replying to the Magistrates said that the defendant was lazy and dirty and the Matron denied the allegation about bread and water rations and said that if a girl is naughty they are not given pudding and they are put on half food. David Love, Probation Officer who had visited the Home and made extensive enquiries, said he spoke to the other girls, and was

assured that they were happy and well fed, and were not made to work very hard. A number of 'old girls' were constantly visiting the Home for weekends.

A.A. was sent to prison for a month and was told she could go back to the Home when she came out.

As the girl was being taken away she gave vent to a hysterical outburst exclaiming, "I'll fight for it; don't worry. I won't go back to the Home. I'll do something to myself."

She was half carried out of court by a wardress and police officers and her cries could be heard for some time." [10]

Another lowlight for the Home was when one of the inmates suddenly confessed to the Matron about killing her mother. Here is the account as it is recorded in the newspaper in 1913;

"Charged on her own confession with giving laudanum to her mother at Gloucester in 1908 with intent to murder her, A.R., single, aged 24, an inmate of Treborth Rescue Home, Cardiff, was at Gloucester on Monday sent for trial. The Matron of Treborth Home said that on 18th June she asked the girl how long her mother had been dead. At first the girl said she could not tell, but afterwards she went and said, "I killed her."

She had it laid on her mind ever since and could not pray. Her sin always came before her.

In her signed statement the accused said, "My mother was drunk in the kitchen. I felt desperate at Mother's treatment, until I thought I would end it. So I went upstairs and took a bottle containing laudanum. This I brought to the kitchen, and when my mother was not looking, I took her glass, carried it to the scullery, and emptied the laudanum into it. I then gave the glass to Mother and said, "Drink this, Mother," and she did so. About two hours afterward she became very ill, and I helped to carry her to bed. She died about ten o' clock. An inquest was held and the verdict was that my mother had taken laudanum herself while she was not in her right mind."

The accused said, "I never knew laudanum was poison till after the inquest, and only thought it was a drug. My mother used to ask my father to give it to her to help her sleep. I thought it would sicken her of drink."

The accused pleaded not guilty and reserved her defence. A.R. was remanded in custody pending further hearings.

At the further hearing, the Matron of Kingswood Treborth Home testified that A R was "somewhat below normal" then the Matron testified that parts of ARs confession were untrue. Namely that A.R. stated that she had thrown her baby into the Gloucester canal when her baby had been delivered at Kingswood Treborth Home and had subsequently died there.

The Judge ruled that she could not be convicted of murder when parts of her confession were found to be false. Therefore the Judge acquitted her and she was discharged into the care of a lady who had found a home for A.R." [11]

Winds of change at the Home

The Kingswood Treborth Home continued in much the same way over the next decade, being supported by various Sisters of the People who often resided at the Home if they were based in that district. Sister Hughes was Deputy Matron for many years (approx 1921 – 1939).

However, the winds of change were beginning to blow, as highlighted by an article in 1931 written by Miss Jefferies, the Matron at the time, who had held the post for ten years, and who was previously one of the Rescue Workers in Bute Street when the work was started twenty-three years previously; and for a while, she was in charge in Grangetown. She wrote as follows;

> "Times have changed since the Kingswood-Treborth home was opened and the girls also in some respects. Never before in the experience of the Matron – have the girls been so difficult to handle and less amenable to discipline. They resent all control and need a constant supervision and this makes the work doubly arduous for the small staff. Then again the buildings need so much repair and these expenses are far too heavy for the number of girls in the Home. Strict economy is practised yet the expenses keep mounting up each year. The Building Committee has already approved of the suggestion for another building for the Home. The Home is not a mere Institution but is made a real home as far as possible, and for some of the girls it is the only true home they have ever known.

> As a denomination we may well be proud of our Home – 80% of the girls become successful." [12]

In 1935, it was reported that the girls and staff moved out of Kingswood Treborth Home for repairs to be undertaken. It was recorded that they were accommodated on a farm near Pyle in South Wales. [13] However, after returning safely to a refurbished Home, they lost their Assistant Matron. In the Treasury February 1939 there is the following tribute to Sister Hughes as she leaves the Home.

> "Miss C A Hughes is a native of Aber (Abergwyngregyn) near Bangor. About 18 years ago she came to Cardiff to undertake duties as a Sister of the People at the Home and during that period she gave most excellent service to the girls in the Home and also as a Sister of the People in the district of Canton, Cardiff.
> She is now entering a new sphere of serving having accepted an invitation to succeed Sister Evans as a Sister of the People at Memorial Hall, Cardiff.
> On Thursday 1st December at its monthly committee meeting a presentation of a cheque and armchair was made to Sister Hughes. The presenter said that Sister Hughes is undoubtedly genial and kind, shedding good influences in whatever sphere she moves. She loves the girls and the girls love her. The Home will miss her and we wish her well and God's richest blessing on her future work" [13a]

However by mid 1940 Sister Hughes was back at the Home as Miss Jeffries, the Matron had resigned, and Sister Hughes became Matron. However in the Treasury September 1941, it is recorded that the Home was partially destroyed by enemy bombing in WW2 [14]. In the Treasury February 1942 it is recorded that Sister Hughes is a Sister of the People at Ely, Cardiff. [14a] It is therefore likely that the Home closed after being partially destroyed.

By 1947, Kingswood Treborth Home was subject to a compulsory requisition by the authorities in Cardiff. [15] Therefore there was active discussion about a replacement Home. The Women's Branch meeting of the Forward Movement in June 1947 recorded that;

"The meeting faced the problem, character, location of the new Home now made necessary by the compulsory requisition of the Kingswood Treborth Home in Cardiff. Full unanimity was expressed in the continuance of the Home and the interests it serves. Much attention was given to the kind of Home it was sought to establish, and ultimately after the elimination of various proposals it was decided to establish a Home which would serve both as a Training Centre for the Sisters of the People and a Centre to which any needy case should find admittance and care. It was suggested that the Home should be in such an area as e.g. Cardiff."[16]

There is no evidence that a new Home was ever built or acquired and this may have been for a number of reasons. Firstly the necessary finances for such a venture may not have been available. Particularly because so much money was required to build new churches on the vast council housing estates that were beginning to spring up all over North and South Wales. Secondly with the introduction of an extended Welfare State in 1948, it was no longer left to churches, denominations and charitable organisations to provide for the welfare needs of the disadvantaged and the vulnerable as this became the responsibility of the State.

<><><><><><>

Chapter Six – Helps & Hindrances

The 1904-5 Revival

The 1904/05 revival undoubtedly empowered and enhanced the effectiveness and progress of the Forward Movement and the Sisters of the People in winning souls for Christ, as a mighty work of the Holy Spirit breezed throughout the land. Rev John Pugh, writing in an article in June 1905 states that the increase in numbers at some of the churches is truly marvellous.

Neath and Pontypool have quadrupled.

Neath has grown from 271 to 1,135 and Pontypool from 30 to 130. Other churches have increased threefold and others have doubled in numbers.

However, Rev John Pugh points out that the increase does not represent the great progress of the Kingdom of God wrought through the Forward Movement, for hundreds of converts join other churches. He cautions against depending too much upon spasmodic revivals, instead of supplying the conditions for a continuous revival.

During the season of revival, he says, "we are all fire and glow, and go; but when the wave of spiritual life has spent itself, we recede back into our former dead level, instead of going in for a fresh supply of divine power by praying and toiling for souls. The result is we become cold and suffer from religious chills.

Let us keep the Fire now kindled by the Spirit of God burning continuously in our churches, by doing His will. For the God 'in whom we live and move and have our being is a 'consuming fire.'

If we keep in the right attitude towards Him and towards our mission to the world, the fire of His Holy Love will never cease to burn in our midst, but will grow in strength and power until, through us, it shall pervade the entire world and fill it with HIS GLORY." [1]

However, following the wonderful breeze of the Holy Spirit seen during the revival years, there were many hindrances to the work in the couple of decades that followed.

World War One

The First World War had a great impact on the work of the Sisters of the People, as they faced the challenge of helping those children who became fatherless, wives who became widows and families that the war had deprived of a bread winner.

In 1914 the following are notes from the diary of one of the Sisters of the People for one month.

Number of hours spent in visiting   130 hours
Number of homes visited   417 homes
Read and prayed in   132 homes
No of sick visits   63 visits
Visited hospital   7 times
I advised 11 to attend church
Conducted 24 women's and other meetings [2]

The war had a huge financial impact on the church, the Forward Movement and the work of the Sisters of the People. In 1914, there is a report of the Forward Movement Directors Meeting where it is recorded;

"We are face-to-face with a deficit to carry on the work."
The deficit is the result of –

(1) Starting five new centres 1913-1914.
(2) Maintaining four Sisters of the People who work so devotedly in the slums of our large towns.
(3) Repaying the loans. [3]

In 1916, the Forward Movement Superintendent writes about the war and its effect on the churches.

"In the meantime, while the conflict is raging, our churches all over the country suffer. The congregations are depleted, whole classes in Sunday School have disappeared and most of our young men, our pride, and our hope, have joined the colours. The condition of the Forward Movement churches in many places, instead of large congregations, that I used to see, there are none now except women and children, and a small sprinkling of men of age. It is a serious question really how to keep the doors open."

Regarding the state of the country, he goes on to say,

"The industrial districts of our country are both morally and spiritually in a terrible state. Notwithstanding all our efforts during the last 25 years, there are more non-church goers and more non-chapel goers in Wales now than when Dr Pugh commenced his great campaign. And the indifference shown by religious men is more appalling than the riotous living of the ungodly." [4]

After the First World War was over and peace returned, the situation in the churches and in the country was little improved.
In 1920, the Superintendent of the Forward Movement writes as follows about the aftermath of the war.

"Never within the memory of man has the land been in such a moral condition as it is at present. Respect for law and order is weakening and under some conditions almost dying out. Crime abounds, impurity is rampant, the effrontery of the unfortunate girls is indescribable and parental control has vanished. In some populous places, hooligans rule, they wantonly destroy property, especially churches and chapels, for the mere gratification of wrongdoing.
As to the attitude of the churches. A large percentage of Christian members imagine that they fulfil the whole law when they attend divine service fairly regularly once a Sunday.
Modern preaching, I am afraid, is not sufficiently vigorous and soul stirring. Carlyle called such preaching the 'treacle gospel.' This sugary, soothing, comforting and palatable gospel, which never makes men conscious of their responsibility and leaves those who listen to it in danger of perishing in their sleep." [5]

The General Strike and the Great Depression

Later in the 1920s there was the General Strike and men were out of work and families really struggled to feed and clothe themselves. There were scenes of such abject and heart-breaking poverty.

Amid such overwhelming circumstances the Sisters of the People endeavoured to carry on their work, often overwhelmed by the need.

In 1928, the Forward Movement Superintendent describes a gift of a large box of bacon sent by Ferme Park Church in London, to help alleviate the distress in the South Wales coalfield, where most of the coal mines had been closed and men were out of work. Many men tramped miles seeking work, but in vain.

The Superintendent describes the work of the Forward Movement and the Sisters of the People in distributing aid to the poverty-stricken families;

> "The other day, I went to a home with a little bundle of clothing. I knew there was poverty in the house, but little did I dream that I was on such an errand of mercy. That day, through the kindness of friends, I was able to clothe almost literally nakedness."

> "Yesterday, some of the bacon sent was taken to a certain home, and whilst there, five little girls came home from school for dinner. Imagine the terrible privations of the home – five little girls sitting down to a dinner of bread and margarine.

> "In the last two days, pieces of bacon have been taken to 74 different homes." [6]

As the 1920s gave way to the 1930s, then the worldwide economic depression struck and exacerbated unemployment in Britain, when one thought it couldn't get any worse. The unemployment rate was well over 40%. Wales was disproportionately affected due to the staple industries of coal, iron and steel. Men were left unable to provide for their families and they had to resort to queueing at the soup kitchens, many organised by the Forward Movement aided by the Sisters of the People, and as many as 600 people could be fed in one day at each soup kitchen.

The situation had a significant impact on the work of the Forward Movement and the Sisters of the People as many people left churches and areas in search of employment. In 1930, the Superintendent of the Forward Movement writes;

> "The Dispersion – we are troubled exceedingly by the fact that increasing numbers have to leave our churches during these years to seek employment elsewhere. The war deprived us of one generation of workers; the long-continued depression will take another. Colonies of young men and women who would prove to be the mainstay of the churches, are being dispersed to London, the Midlands, the North and across the seas in search of work." [6a]

In the Treasury August 1936, the Superintendent of the Forward Movement summed it all up by saying;

> "So, these obstacles of unemployment and cruel poverty are massed in mighty array – all producing the feeling in the hearts of ordinary decent folk, that religion is irrelevant to their needs and problems. But what people need is the Gospel – good news," and the Sisters of the People endeavoured, against all odds to bring that good news to the people and to show them the love of Christ in action. [7]

In the following chapter there are reports from some of the Sisters of the People during these very difficult, challenging and trying years.

<><><><><><>

Chapter Seven – Blood, Sweat, Toil and Tears – Sisters Reports from the Inter-War Years

The Gorse Chapel Cwmbwrla, Swansea

During the 1904-5 revival members of Babell Chapel, Cwmbwrla felt led to a dark and dismal area called Gorse Road. The Cwmbwrla Tin Plate works were based there and they gave permission for an unused wood and tin shed, fondly known as the 'Black Shed' to be used as a place for families and children of the area to worship and learn more about Jesus. The Black Shed was replaced by a permanent building, The Gorse Mission Hall that opened in 1926. It continued until 2022 when the lease expired, and there is a planning application pending to replace it with residential flats.

In 1924, Sister Margaret Jones gives a report on her work from The Black Shed

> "I have tried my utmost to keep in touch with the people, visiting them daily in their homes. I find very often the people will open up their hearts to the Sister, telling her all about their troubles. When possible, we have a prayer offered and that brings comfort. When there is death in the family we can touch their hearts, and many have been won this way to attend the Mission. When the people have anyone belonging to them in hospital, I endeavour to visit them, and they greatly appreciate that. We have meetings every night except Saturday in The Mission and I am always present. Our Christian Endeavour has been a source of blessing to our young people. There seems to me that there is a thirst in their souls for the Living Water. I find that personal evangelism is a successful means of winning souls for the Master. After the Sunday Evening Service, I have a personal talk with individuals, and it has been my joy lately to lead seven young people to the Saviour in this way. I take the service every Sunday morning, and also in the evening every six weeks. I have two Bible Classes weekly, and I have a Sunday School class.

The tasks are not always sweet, sometimes it's hard, but I leave everything in His hands." [8]

Clydach-on-Tawe, Swansea

The work started in 1917 on 'Pub' premises and the Forward Movement church was opened in 1921. It is still a functioning, flourishing church today.

In 1924, Sister Lydia gives a report of her work at Clydach-On-Tawe, she writes;

> "This is now my fourth year in the Centre and I am glad to say it has been a happy time of service. The work certainly has not been free from difficulties, disappointments and discouragements, but a joy in knowing that when He calls, He undertakes, 'God never, never fails.' I have known what it is to work in the slums in my training days, but never found it so hard as I find it these days. I often find that people are too respectable to reach. They are so satisfied with themselves. It is really like preaching forgiveness, often to people who have not felt the need for it. Most of the people here have not been accustomed to church going, oft times they come as a result of our visiting. Then we have our young people and their demand for entertainment. We meet them through their own meetings. With respect to the demand of the children which is the greatest because they are the future of the Church. We meet them through Children's Services on Sundays as well as weekdays. I do pray the Lord to use me here in this village. He has really shown me that to satisfy Him is to be the first object of my life, that I must share His distress for His unfruitful children, and that my 'love' service must always bring Him more advantage than 'duty' service and that the most important part of that service from His point of view, is my 'prayer' life."

Sister Lydia was shortly to be transferred to serve at the Marshes Newport, Monmouthshire. [9]

Grove Place, Morriston

Meetings started in a tin shed until the Mission Hall at Grove Place was built. Sister Alison Jones was there for 42 years and here is her very encouraging report from 1924. Sadly, the Mission Hall closed several years ago and is now residential accommodation.

She writes;

> "Grove Place district is completely changed by the Grace of God. We have been admitted practically into every home and welcomed there. I have visited about 100 homes per week, sometimes more, besides visits paid to Swansea Hospital and also the Workhouse. God has blessed my efforts amongst the children, I have won nearly all of them to love God's house and too often out little church is far too small to hold them. Then the women's meetings have been specially blessed, many have been brought in as members, finding the Saviour, and accepting Him in our Women's Gospel Meeting.
>
> Cottage prayer meetings in the homes of people are held each week, these are greatly appreciated and owned of God in a wonderful way.
>
> I find the personal visits pay well, getting into the homes and first, leading dear ones to the Lord on their own hearthstones. I sometimes wish I had more strength and more money.
>
> Sometimes they need a meal or a garment before I can offer them 'The Bread of Life' and the 'Robe of Righteousness.'
>
> I had been calling for a long time to get a dear man to the service, he had been out of work for months. Of course, he said 'I have no clothes, Sister, no coat.' I mentioned the case and a Brother said to me, 'I will lend you my overcoat for him if he will come.' He came that night in the borrowed overcoat and found the 'Pearl of Great Price.' I had the joy of leading him personally to Christ. I have to take most of the meetings myself in the church. I am superintendent of the Sunday School, Band of Hope, and also Children's Service, very often speaker as well, and find often the

work very hard, but I love it for the sake of Him, who did so much for me." [9a]

The Burrows, Swansea

The Burrows was near the docks area in Swansea, very vulnerable to enemy bombing during the war years and described as one of the "darkest parts of the town" The work was established as an outreach from Port Tennant church Sister Esther gives a report of her work at The Burrows, in March 1924.

She writes;

> "In reviewing the work of the past year, one cannot but utter 'Praise God' what a marvel of grace that we are still alive and well, with a sphere of usefulness open to us.
>
> Services, meetings and classes have been held every week with unfailing regularity and attendance has been good. I have found the past year a difficult one. There appears to be a hardness in these days, which is more manifest today than even a year ago. Nevertheless, conversions have steadily followed the preaching of the Word, and I rejoice in the privilege of making known the Gospel of Christ. Personal and constant visitation is the great need of our district. I have endeavoured to keep in close touch with our flock, and also to do house to house visitation. In this way I get in touch with the people and get to know the conditions under which many of them live, and it is surprising how they appreciate the visits and are intensely grateful for the cups of cold-water God enables us to minister for His name's sake. The cup of cold water means sometimes sitting up with a sick one in order to win a mother or father, or seeking a dear sister or brother, who has wandered far in sin.
>
> Our Mother's Meeting is greatly appreciated and well attended. The Girl's Meeting, held every Thursday, has an attendance of 30 to 40.
>
> During the summer, we had open air services, and it is an inspiring sight to see our young people taking active part and testifying to the saving and keeping power of Jesus. [10]

Memorial Hall, Cardiff

This was the jewel in the Forward Movement crown. The work started in a tent in Neville Street, then in a wooden shed, and then in an upper room above an undertakers workshop. The splendid church building, named in memory of David Davies of Llandinam (a great benefactor to the Forward Movement) opened in 1893.
Sister Evans gives a report of her work at Memorial Hall, Cardiff in April 1924, She was the widow of the late Rev Ben Evans of Garston, who died at an early age. Sister Evans took over from Sister White, who was at Memorial Hall for a few years from 1920. [10a]

She writes;

> "I will give my impression of the Sister's work during the last year. It is difficult for me to speak of one's own work, so I say here 'of myself I can do nothing' but by surrender of myself to be used of God, I know much can be done. Yet it is difficult to tabulate the results of spiritual work as undesirable in the case of a Sister as in that of a Minister. Figures vary and cannot tell the true worth of work done e.g. I have visited 45 houses in a week, the next perhaps 10 and yet done more in that week for the Kingdom.
>
> This is my day – from 9:00 – 12:30 in my room for Bible study and prayer that I may be made fit to meet all that comes in my way. From 1:00 – 5:00 visiting or attending various meetings as the case may be. Then tea, rest and study until 7:00. Then in the hall, mostly taking part, one way or another, until 9:00/9:30 every day except Friday, when I have no meetings in the evening. Saturday is a day for rest and study.
>
> I marvel at the gratitude and love of the people. Only the consecrated life, the knowledge it is a task given of God, to whom I must give an account daily, will keep me at it faithfully, sowing beside all waters, never thinking of myself. It is a lovely life, but I always go home dead tired. I see miracles done often and my work makes it easier to believe. So I go on, not in my feeble hold, but in His mighty grasp of me." [11]

Eastmoors Hall, Cardiff

In August 1928, a startling new venture was started at Eastmoors Hall, the first Forward Movement Hall that opened under Rev John Pugh in 1892.

The church members and congregation from Eastmoors moved to Jerusalem Chapel, Splott, Cardiff, a short distance away and Eastmoors Forward Movement Church was turned into an Institute, under the charge of Sister Elsie Hole, assisted by a council of influential citizens of Cardiff. This was a unique and innovative work for a Sister of the People.

There were two departments –

    Girls (junior and senior)
    Boys (junior and senior)

The Institute offered gymnasium exercises, needlework, raffia and basket work, Red Cross, Girl Guides and singing classes.

Some of the benefits were thought to be –
   i.   effective way of gathering the youth from the streets of Splott
   ii.   it was the only Institute in the Splott area;
   iii.   Institute works assists church work in trying to get youths to church.

Sister Elsie reports that gangs of boys who were at a loose end and prowling the streets are now under training within the Institute.

Memberships as follows (excluding Girl Guides, Brownies and Boys Brigade) –

Males Senior	203
Males Junior	50
Female Senior	25
Female Junior	50 [12]

In 1933, Sister Elsie reports on the Children's Sunday Evening Gospel Service, another innovative outreach organised by Sister Elsie Hole at Splott Institute (previously Eastmoor Forward Movement Hall).

Sister Elsie writes as follows;

> "This important branch of our work in this area is carried on under great difficulties by a small band of workers. The majority of the children attending these services are from homes where little, if any, parental authority is exercised. They are left to run wild about the streets, and therefore, when gathered together in any place, are very unruly. We have had great difficulty this session to run our services as successfully as we did last year, owing to the formation of gangs amongst the children, especially the boys.
>
> Previously we could deal with the individual, now, we have to deal with gangs, for as gangs they come. We have one gang of boys between the ages of 13 and 15 whose sole aim from the beginning was to disturb the services. At first we felt like refusing them admission, then we realised that after all this was the type of boy we were out to capture. Miss Gwen Jones volunteered to take this great task in hand and deals with them in a room of their own every Sunday evening.
>
> The service is carried on by the children, a boy and a girl presiding alternatively, the prayer, the reading and special items are also taken by the children. The workers give the address with occasional outside speakers. The children are very fond of singing, so we have as much signing as possible in our programme. Though the children are so unruly and makes one think that they do not want the services, when it was suggested to discontinue them, they voted unanimously against the suggestion. So we have decided to carry on the good work in spite of the difficulties." [13]

Kingsway Hall, Cardiff

The work in the Cathays area of Cardiff started in a room over a stables in Dalcross Street. It later moved to premises in Fitzroy street (1898), which were previously occupied by a Drinking Club. In the 1930's the facilities at the Fitzroy Street Mission became increasingly inadequate and so it closed and the congregation took over the more spacious Kingsway Hall (previously a Mission Hall for the Presbyterian Church of England)

Here is an abstract from the report for 1934 for the Kingsway Hall, shortly after they moved to their new premises, and written by Sister Watkins;

> **Visiting The Homes** – This work affords endless opportunities . Here one gets to know the people, their strengths, sorrows and fears and in the heart-to-heart talk, one can bring in the message of the Great Burden Bearer who said, 'come unto me all that labour and are heavy laden, and I will give you rest.' What a rich, glorious gospel, with a message for all!
>
> **The work in the open air** – There are many who are opposed to the churches and chapels, but willing to hear the gospel message on their own doorsteps in the open air. Our first concern is not getting them into any particular hall or chapel but to get the gospel lodged in their hearts. To this end tracts and testaments are given out and sometimes there is an opportunity for personal work. The power of evil and its effects are felt and seen all around us, so we take advantage of this means of bearing witness to another power - the gospel that is able to save and to lift – and we freely praise God in the open street.
>
> **The work amongst women** – There are many in the district that never go to any place of worship and while it would be fruitless to try and get them into the Sunday services, some are persuaded to come to the Women's Meeting. This is a bright gospel meeting and we ask prayer that as the message is given these women will come in touch with Him who brings salvation, healing and rest to the human heart." [14]

Thus the turbulent years of the First World War the General Strike, and the great economic Depression were overshadowed by the beginning of World War Two in 1939. The Sisters of the People continued their work during the war period. Sister Alison Jones was at Morriston, Sister Kate Thomas was at Trethomas, Sister Watkins was at Kingsway Hall. Sister Elsie Hole was at Eastmoor, near to the Steelworks, a veritable target for enemy bombing. Thus they continued their faithful service, but little is written about this period in the reference sources.

<><><><><><>

Chapter Eight – A New Vision for a New Era

At the end of World War Two, peoples' immediate concerns were somewhere to live. Bombing during the war was estimated to have destroyed well over 500,000 homes and many more were left significantly damaged. Even before the war, many homes needed modernisation. Many did not have an indoor toilet, a bathroom or even hot water and many were cold and damp. There was such a shortage of accommodation that may families ended up living in one room in relative's or stranger's homes, where they lived, ate and slept, all in the same room.

The Government attempted to solve these issues by building over a million new homes over an extended period. Eighty percent of these were council houses built by the local councils to be rented to families. As there was a shortage of both building materials and skilled labour, coupled with the urgent need, a significant number of homes were prefabricated, steel framed, or of concrete slab construction, so that homes could be produced quickly. But still demand way outstripped supply.

Thus the councils up and down Wales were committed to building vast numbers of houses, which turned into vast council housing estates, mostly on the periphery of the towns and cities.

For example, in Cardiff, building took place in Fairwater, Gabalfa, Ely, Llanishen and Rumney.

In Monmouthshire there were plans for estates in Ringland and Malpas Court in Newport and 35,000 houses on seven estates in Cwmbran and also the Hilltops estate between Ebbw Vale and Beaufort.

In West Glamorgan there were plans for 16,000 houses at Port Talbot to accommodate families of the steelworkers. This was later renamed The Sandfields Estate.

There was the Gorof Estate in Cwmtwrch, Swansea, the Hengwrt Estate in Briton Ferry and the Felinfoel and Brynsierfel estates in Llanelli.

Further north there was Gil Peblig Estate near Caernarvon, Morfa Bach Estate in Rhyl, vast estates in Bangor, Maesgeirchen and Ffriddoedd and also the trading estate at Wrexham.

In 1947, the President of the Forward Movement, Rev E Lewis Mendus drafted an article on the "New Venture of the Forward Movement."

Here he highlighted the task given to the Forward Movement by the Reconstruction Committee of the denomination namely;

> "to establish new churches and secure new sites and adequate (but not too costly) buildings. This has to be done in close consultation with the Presbytery Committee, but also in harmony with plans of other denominations and with the town planning arrangements in those areas. Also
>
> - to watch the transference of populations in Wales and outside of it; and
> - to supervise and maintain Evangelists and Sisters of the People and arrange pastoral oversight and financial support." [1]

In 1948, The President of the Forward Movement writes;

> "At the express invitation of the Presbytery I visited the new housing estates outside Caernarvon and at Orrell (Liverpool). Cardiff Corporation is contemplating new estates of about 1,000 houses each at Ely, Gabalfa, Rumney and Fairwater and the Forward Movement have claimed sites for centres in three of these new areas.
>
> These are only a small percentage of the great number of new housing estates that are springing up in North and South Wales. The challenge is tremendous but the time is short, God says 'today,' tomorrow the opportunity may be gone forever. The need is still labourers for the vineyard." [2]

Thus the Forward Movement seized the vision to build new churches on many of these vast new housing estates. Thus it was as if the work was starting afresh. As many of the churches built at the turn of the century under the pioneering work and vision of Rev John Pugh were no longer at the epicentres of the population, as depopulation was taking place, as vast swathes of people were moving to new council housing estates.

The Sisters of the People faced completely different challenges, as there was increasing affluence and materialism amongst people. Technology was making great strides, in transport, working class families were obtaining cars. Household appliances flooded the market, washing machines, fridges, freezers etc. There were widespread government subsidies in post-war education, young people could go to college for next to nothing.

In 1957, Prime Minister Harold Macmillan summed it all up by saying, "You've never had it so good".

Rev Ieuan Phillips, Superintendent of the Forward Movement, commented;

> "The circumstances in Wales have altered greatly, but the essentials are the same. John Pugh went to people in dire poverty when living conditions were so squalid that they were glad to be welcomed into commodious, well heated and well lighted Halls. Today we preach to people in affluent circumstances.
>
> Teenagers as well as adults have money and all that money can buy, but these conditions are only the obverse and reverse sides of the same coin namely man's desperate need of salvation" [2a]

However, there were long delays in councils approving sites and plans for new churches. Also finance became a limiting factor as the need for new churches was so great.

The General Assembly of the Presbyterian Church of Wales set up a committee in 1951 to find ways and means of securing adequate finances for the Forward Movement work in new areas and very substantial sums of money would have to be secured. Amongst the suggestions was that the Church Assembly authorise an immediate appeal for a fund of £30,000 [3] (in today's value that would be over 1.2 million pounds) – this was the size of the task they were facing to have new churches on the vast number of new housing estates springing up across Wales, and in 1955, the Superintendent of the Forward Movement states,

> "Whilst naturally we feel the challenge of the new areas and have sought to secure sites and erect halls/churches, we feel the greatest of our problems is to secure devoted men and women to labour in them." [4]

Annie Pugh Williams (daughter of John Pugh) and Organiser of the work of the Sisters of People, writes in the April 1959 Home Mission News Sheet of the Presbyterian Church of Wales as follows;

> "I have spent some time recently touring North and South Wales, viewing the new housing estates and was shocked and distressed to find there was no spiritual provision made in many of them.
> A third of the population of Wales are being moved into new housing areas. Experience has proved that if the Church is there with the houses, 70% or 80% of the new population may be brought within the fellowship; but if the church is 10 years late, that figure may drop to 10%.
> Remember the famous words of Robert Moffat that set David Livingstone's heart on fire, 'I have often stood and watched the smoke rise from a thousand villages where no missionary has ever been.' Livingstone vowed that to these and thousands more, God helping him, he would bring the Gospel. Not in darkest Africa only, but in the dark places of our own land must this light shine. That is the urgent challenge of the hour. The night is far spent, delay cripples our faith." [4a]

Thus the Forward Movement faced the huge challenge of translating into reality its vision for new churches on the vast new Council housing estates being established across Wales. However this challenge was no bigger than the challenge faced by John Pugh at the beginning of the Forward Movement work in 1891. By the time of his death in 1907, John Pugh had overseen the building and establishment of 48 new churches, in just 16 years. Find out in the next two chapters how the new vision unfolded for the Forward Movement and the work of the Sisters of the People.

<><><><><><><>

Chapter Nine – New Beginnings – North Wales

There were early beginnings for the work of the Sisters of the People in North Wales. In 1907, Sister Elizabeth Jones from Pwllheli was based at Victoria Hall, Wrexham. [5]

Sister Margaret Jones commenced work at Caernarvon in 1919. She then came to South Wales and founded the Gorse Mission Hall at Cwmbwrla, which opened in 1926.

Victoria Hall, Wrexham

In the Treasury October 1953, Mrs Ezekiel Williams (Beatrice) is appointed Sister of the People at Victoria Hall, Wrexham after the death of her husband the Minister in 1952. She was Sister in charge and carried out the majority of the duties her husband, the Minister would have done previously. [6]

In 1960, Sister Beatrice Williams was awarded an MBE for her services to religion in the Wrexham area. In November 1960 Victoria Hall moved to Bersham Road, and thereafter to Hampden Road. [7] Sister Beatrice Williams retired in 1965.

Trinity, Lay, Wrexham

In 1961 Trinity, Lay, Wrexham was without a Pastor and Sister Thelma Pope was appointed as Sister in Charge. [8]

In 1964, Sister Mair Jones is at Trinity, Lay, Wrexham as Sister in Charge. [9]

She completed her training in 1954 at Ridgelands and previously served at Markham, South Wales and Gorof, Cwmtwrch. The Gorof is a large housing estate built to house the workers at the large clock factory.

Trinity opened in November 1922, but by the late 1960s numbers were declining, so in 1969 Trinity was sold and members transferred to Glanabar. [10]

Maesgeirchen, Bangor

Sister Mary Williams joined the Forward Movement as a Sister of the People in 1948. She trained in Porth Bible College under Rev R B Jones. For many years she was the Matron in Charge of Llety Cranogwen, Tonypandy (a shelter for homeless women and girls opened in 1922 by the South Wales Temperance Union). Sister Williams' first assignment was Maesgeirchen housing estate in Bangor. She was the pioneer who commenced the work there and largely on her report the Forward Movement Board decided to erect a chapel. After a year she was asked to go to Pendine, South Wales, to do similar work. In 1949 she was appointed Sister of the People at Mount Pleasant, Ely, Cardiff and worked there with marked success for four years. [11] Her story is continued on Page 76.

Penllyn, Llangollen

In 1967 Miss E K Avery from Penllyn, Llangollen where there is a small Mission Hall in the housing estate was the Sister in Charge working amongst the children. Miss Avery was a trained teacher. [14]

Morfa Bach and Mill Bank, Rhyl

Sister Gwen Morrow was appointed as a Sister of the People to serve the church at Ruabon.

'A new Sister a new sphere,' Rhyl was the new sphere of Forward Movement activities and was the first sphere accepted for service by Sister Gwen Morrow (after probationary work at Ruabon), Clwyd Street Church placed at the disposal of the work, two mission centres – Morfa Bach and Mill Bank. Sister Gwen began her work there in October 1946. [15]

Cil Peblig, Caernarvon

In 1955 Emily Roberts was appointed as a Sister of the People at Caernarvon.

> "Miss Emily Roberts, Llanmawddwy trained as a teacher and is already working amongst children and young people. We hope to announce her appointment soon." [16]

> "Caernarvon – Cil Peblig – Sister Emily Roberts has worked for some months in this new estate. Over 400 houses have already been visited. A benefactor has paid for the land and for a temporary Mission building is to be erected." [17]

Sister Emily started off working without a building, gathering children and taking them to the Presbyterian chapels in town for services and Band of Hope etc. But she soon realised that the most effective way to work would be if she could form a mission project on the estate. And so a second-hand chapel was acquired – the old Methodist chapel from Porthmadog. Sister Emily arranged for it to be moved on trailers to Caernarvon and erected on the Ysgubor Goch Estate in 1956, and this was now her Mission centre covering the local housing estates of Maes Barcer, Coed Marion and Ysgubor Goch. As it was the 150th anniversary of Ann Griffiths death the building was called 'Noddfa' apparently because that name appeared in some of her hymns.

Over the following years the work flourished and Sister Emily had the vision to establish a church on the estate. With the help of local residents and the Presbyterian Church of Wales, they raised enough money to build a permanent, brick-built church (the other building being made of metal) and the new chapel at Cil Peblig was opened on the 30th of September 1965 [18a] The new church was built on the existing site, and included a chapel to seat 300, a vestry and five Sunday School classrooms, a Minister's Office, a kitchen and boiler room and a vestibule. The chapel had a forty-foot tower with a cross on it. [18b] The church would also serve the newly built Ty Gwyn Estate.

During that time, three services were held every Sunday and many children attended the Sunday School and Band of Hope. Sister Emily was devoted to the area and the people, beside evangelism, she offered practical help and support for local residents.

An insight into the work at Cil Peblig, Caernarvon from Sister Emily Roberts

Here in Sister Emily's own words is a typical day in her life (Glad Tidings April 1968);

> "My custom is to spend some time before breakfast in reading the Word of God and in prayer. Seeking to meet with God before meeting with anyone else, but sometimes I am called to a home even before breakfast.

I cannot always be sure of spending a whole night in bed but have to remain by the bedside of some sick person, and sometimes stay with them until they have 'crossed the flood.'

On a normal morning, I glance at the daily paper and then attend to correspondence. There are usually a pile of letters, and in their midst many forms to be filled or a letter from a works manager wanting a testimonial to the character of someone from the district seeking work. 'Someone from the chapel' you may think so, but very infrequently, for it is only a minority on this vast estate, but when they want something their cry is, 'I am sure Sister will do it.'

In the midst of attending to my correspondence or preparing for a service in the chapel that same evening, there will be a knock on the door, someone wanting to share a problem, asking for advice or wanting some favour or other – or sometimes 'please come at once – he or she is desperately ill.'

This happened today and I have to leave this report and go at once to see the woman to whom I called the doctor – and also telephone Ambulance Control to see whether they have made the necessary arrangements to take Mrs Jones to see the specialist in Liverpool tomorrow. While I am out I call to see Mrs Evans who is lonely and with no one to care for her but who will not hear of any suggestion that she should go to an old people's home. What ought I to do?

But it's lunchtime. It is not unusual for me to spend the morning in court, before the Bench, arguing the case for some wrongdoer from the area, or in one of the offices of the Welfare State, mediating on behalf of families in trouble or need. Is not a Sister of the People a link between the people and the Church, and between the people and the Welfare State? For despite the benefits of the Welfare State, one still finds children and old people who are wronged, large families living in tiny houses, while the unemployed and lazy gather on street corners; one finds loneliness, and wantonness, drunkenness and broken marriages. The Welfare State doesn't offer and doesn't pretend to offer a satisfactory answer to every problem. The heart of the trouble is the trouble of the heart, and only the Gospel – only Jesus Christ – can deal effectively with this. How many people have I tried to persuade that their only hope lies in their conversion and tried to induce them to turn to Jesus Christ and lead them along the road to salvation. This is the main aim and purpose of every visit, every kindness and every favour performed both within the church an outside it.

Visiting, that's what I usually do after lunch – visit people in hospital and the old and lonely in their homes and it makes no difference whether or not they worship at Noddfa, although I do try not to impose on members of other chapels who live in my area, except to let their Minister know if something is wrong.

The people of Noddfa and the people of no place of worship are my people. I may say a verse in one place, sing a hymn in another, read a Psalm, or say a word of prayer, as the opportunity arises, and always trying to create an atmosphere which makes another visit easy and natural.

The social work necessitates keeping in close contact with the clerk of the Town Council and the Councillors, the Housing Committee, The Probation Officer, the Childcare Officer, as well as the Employment Bureau. A Sister of the People is known to doctors and nurses, to the police, the WVS, the Red Cross and other organisations. There is the occasional case for the NSPCC and even the RSPCA sometimes. I will never forget the trouble I had to persuade an old un-cared for woman to let me ask the RSPCA to put her even more un-cared for cat to sleep. But these acts are all the means to another end. Through every fire kindled, every cup of tea brewed, every present taken to the sick, every person helped, through all that is done for them and on their behalf – behind all this is the desire to speak for Him, to open people's eyes to their greatest need and to persuade them to accept Jesus as their Saviour and Lord.

Although there are three or four meetings to prepare during the week, and three and sometimes four on a Sunday, many a morning slips by without my having been in the study or out visiting people.

I must officiate at weddings and funerals. Tomorrow there are two funerals – no, not of chapel members, but an opportunity nevertheless to help to evangelise and induce the living to, 'count their days' and to prepare themselves to face the same journey.

Next week I shall be spending the greatest part of one day in the Presbytery, and on one evening there is a meeting of the Council of Evangelical Churches of the town, while on Saturday afternoon, the Women's Auxiliary is meeting. Glancing at the calendar, I notice one week where I am committed to attend six meetings and committees apart from those of the church, which are in my care and my usual everyday work.

Fortunately, I do not have to go to address any rallies or auxiliaries that week.

It is very difficult to fit in the normal work at home when I am away addressing meetings, and indeed it requires a whole morning or afternoon to write a report like this, without considering the time it takes to prepare it beforehand.

There's the phone ringing. It's nearly 10 o'clock at night, 'could you go and tell Mam that I've reached Liverpool safely?" Of course I'll go. Then back. I read a little of the Word and say a word of prayer.

Entrusting everyone with whom we have been in contact during the day to His care, putting our troubles before Him, with every meeting in which we have been involved – and then to bed.

I know of homes in this area where there is not enough room for the children to sleep comfortably, nor clean clothes on the bed.

I know that there are five children 'next door' whose parents are in the pub.

I know of a family who have neither gas nor electricity because they have not paid their bills.

I know that several of the children will be in court on Monday.

I know that a certain man is in goal.

I know that a certain girl has run away to London and tomorrow I must get in touch with the London City Mission.

I know another girl who is unmarried and will soon give birth to a child.

I know very well that few people want the church, although they are all in need. But I know also that Jesus Christ died for them and loves them still. That is why it is essential to carry on despite the cost. That is why I am able to fall asleep presently with a peaceful mind. That is why I can wake up in the morning, if He wills it, ready to continue my mission and evangelical work, trying through the power of the Holy spirit, to open the eyes of the blind, to their need of Jesus Christ, whom to know is life indeed. [19]

Unfortunately, by the 1980s there was a national decline in church numbers and Noddfa was facing financial difficulties and in the mid-1980s the building was transferred to the County Council, to be used for the county's community work on the written understanding that the church had full use of the building on Sundays.

After Sister Emily left Noddfa, the mission board of the Presbyterian Church of Wales had the vision to place mission workers at Noddfa.

Today there are still church Community workers at Noddfa. There are services every Sunday and a faithful small congregation.

The church still reaches out to the community to offer support in very much the same way as Sister Emily did.

Find out in the next chapter the new beginnings for the work of the Sisters of the People in South Wales.

<><><><><><>

Chapter Ten – New Beginnings – South Wales

Sandfields, Port Talbot

In March 1948, it is recorded that Sister Gwen Morrow is to join Sister Kate at Trethomas, as she feels she would like to have experience in the industrial towns of South Wales. [20]

Then in September 1949 it is recorded that Sister Gwen Morrow commenced work in a new sphere. A large new housing estate has sprung up in Sandfields, Port Talbot and she will work there. This area was probably the largest new suburb in Wales, connected with the project of the Steel company of Wales and with a population of 16,000. [21]

In 1955 it is reported that the local authority had consented to sell land for the erection of a church on the new estate of Sandfields. [22]

Whilst waiting for the allocation of land by the Council, Sister Gwen had already commenced work, a very large Sunday School met in the Glan Y Mor School, rented from the Council. Weeknight meetings were also held in the school, Open air meetings also took place and in conjunction with volunteers from Bethlehem Church, the whole estate was visited. Sister Gwen was under the guidance of Rev J Thomas from Bethlehem.

In June 1959, it is reported that at last Fitzclarence Hall, Sandfields, Port Talbot was opened on the 25th of June 1959, seating 450 people. Dr Martyn Lloyd Jones preached the inaugural sermon. [23]

Sunday schools held in Glan y Mor School prior to the opening of the church were seeing over 250 children attending. Rev W Stead was appointed minister at Fitzclarence in 1961 and was minister there for 55 years.

Thanks to Miss Mary Lody of Bethlehem Church, Port Talbot for providing some of this information.

Llanelli

In September 1949, it is reported that;

> "A young lady called Morwen Thomas of Brynea, Llanelli has been accepted on probation as a Sister of the People and she will go to Sister Kate at Trethomas early in September to commence her training." [24]

In February 1950 it is reported as follows;

> "Our youngest recruit to the ranks of Sisters of the People has spent a profitable time under Sister Kate at Trethomas. She has now been accepted as a student at Ridgelands Bible College, Bexley, Kent. The course is for two years." [25]

It was reported in 1952 that Sister Morwen had completed her training and gained a diploma, and that she was working on the new housing estate of Brynsherfal, Llanelli and that there was a site acquired and plans in place for a new Hall. However, there were to be long delays with the new Hall. [26]

Sister Morwen reported in March 1953;

> "there is a decided increase in those attending services. Sunday evenings 30-40 adults and 50-60 children." [27]

Morena Griffiths, after training at Ridgelands Bible College, joined Sister Morwen in the work at Brynsherfel, Llanelli.

Finally, the hall at Brynsherfel, Llanelli was opened on the 9th of May 1955. At the opening;

> "Sister Morwen spoke from a full heart. She said that this was not a new church, the people had begun to come in, but likened their feelings to people cramped in an apartment, suddenly moving into a beautiful new home of their own." [28]

There are several records of Sister Morwen speaking very powerfully at Women's Conferences. However, in 1955, Sister Morwen Thomas terminated her engagement with the Forward Movement as a Sister of the People. She married the Rev W Vernon Higham and together they had a powerful and faithful ministry over many years, which was richly blessed.

Also working in Llanelli at Felinfoel and Llwynhendy estates (based at Salem Felinfoel), was Sister Gladys Rees. In July 1952 it is reported;

> "After a long period of hard work, this centre under Sister Gladys Rees is showing marked signs of revival. People have commenced coming from the neighbouring estates. A few Sundays ago, there were nearly 100 adults present at the Sunday evening service." [29]

However, in 1953 Sister Gladys Rees terminated her work with the Forward Movement and later married Mr Wyndham Lewis from Llanelli.

Malpas Court, Newport, South Wales

Kathleen Walker of Hove, Sussex was accepted as a Sister of the People at the beginning of March 1957. She trained at Ridgelands Bible College and has been allocated to work on the Malpas Court Estate. [30] A new church was proposed for the estate, but her temporary base was Malpas Road Church. The new church on the Malpas Court Estate was finally opened on the 18th of May 1961. There is a record in the Treasury of vandalism at the church, where all the windows were broken.

Writing in the Treasury in 1961, Rev David Owen reports on the work at Malpas Court as follows;

> "We are in the midst of a huge population at Malpas Court, yet in all my ministry I have never found it harder. On the other hand there is encouragement when we look around us. The people who come to this estate are very kind and gracious and there is always an open door and a real welcome. The only method that used to be a real success was by visiting the homes, but today it is not so for there are many difficulties facing such visitations. Shift work, the TV set and of course cars have made it possible to get out and away at weekends. In spite of these

obvious difficulties, they only strengthen our resolve to continue in faith and perseverance and to keep on attacking the problems facing us. Difficulties are ladders for the church of today." [31]

In 1962, it is recorded that Sister Kathleen Walker, after moving from Malpas Court to Port Tennant resigned from being a Sister of the People due to illness. [32]

Hilltops Estate, Ebbw Vale

In November 1950, Sister May Markey leaves Trethomas to undertake duties in co-operation with Mount Pleasant Church, on the large new housing estate which was being erected between Ebbw Vale and Beaufort (Hilltops). [33]

In August 1951, Sister May Markey was transferred to the centre at Markham and friends at Mount Pleasant kindly promised to supervise the work commenced on the new estate by Sister Markey, pending the erection of a church. [34]

In 1954, Sister May Markey moved to the work at Lower Gelli [35] and in September 1955, sister May Markey terminated her position with the Forward Movement. [36]

The church at Hilltops Estate, Ebbw Vale was eventually opened on the 24th of July 1963.

Mount Pleasant, Ely, Cardiff

In 1949 Sister Mary Williams was appointed sister of the People at Mount Pleasant, Ely, Cardiff and worked there with marked success for four years. [37]

Whilst at Mount Pleasant, she suffered health problems and was in St David's Hospital, Cardiff for over a month. This came at a time when she was beginning to see fruit for her very hard labour. After discharge from St David's Hospital by the kindness of Miss Margaret Davies, Gregynog (granddaughter of David Davies, a great benefactor of the Forward Movement) she was invited to Bronhaul, Llandinam for two weeks convalescence and it greatly benefitted her.[38]

Following that, a worker was urgently needed in Sarn (Ystradgynlais) and Sister Mary volunteered to go there. After three years there, she went to Trethomas on the retirement of Sister Kate. She ministered at Trethomas for six years, greatly beloved and respected by the whole community. In 1962 she was appointed to Port Tennant, Swansea where se worked until the end of August 1964. Though retired from the active list of Sisters, Sister Mary intimated her readiness to serve the Forward Movement and churches in a part time capacity.[39]

Bethel, Heol Trelai, Caerau, Ely, Cardiff

Sister Margaret Hayes was Sister of the People at Bethel, Caerau, Cardiff for many years.

In the Treasury April 1956, it is announced that Margaret Hayes, who was a member of Memorial Hall Church, Canton, had expressed her desire to be a Sister of the People. She did two years training at Ridgelands College and during the holidays from college, she worked as a student probationer at Kingsway Hall, Cardiff.

After qualifying from Bible College, Sister Margaret worked on the Gorof Estate in Lower Cwmtwrch. It was a large new estate and there was a new prefabricated hall, which opened in June 1954. [40]

In 1960, Sister Margaret Hayes was moved to Broadway Church, Sketty, [41] and from there, Sister Margaret Hayes was placed at the newly opened Bethal Church in Caerau, Ely, Cardiff where she was to work for many years.

Gabalfa Hall, Gabalfa, Cardiff

At the annual women's meeting of the Forward Movement held at Shrewsbury in November 1956, the delegates were asked to interview a young lady from Liverpool, Miss Joyce Dowber, who was applying for training as a Sister of the People. She was introduced by Mrs Ann Pugh-Williams. Miss Dowber then spoke and gave her spiritual experience and her call to full time work. After hearing her speak the meeting unanimously decided to accept her for training as a probationer. [42]

Joyce was sent under the auspices of the Forward Movement to Ridgelands Bible College in Kent in 1958 for two years of training.

In 1960, it is recorded that Joyce had finished her training at Ridgelands and was assigned as Sister of the People at the newly opened hall in Gabalfa, Cardiff.[43]

The Treasury records that the Gabalfa Hall opened on the 6th of December 1959 and that Sister Heulwen Jones covered Gabalfa Hall in the first few months, as well as Kingsway Hall, Cardiff. She was assisted by a band of workers drawn from Heath Church. [44]

Within weeks of Sister Joyce arriving at Gabalfa, the estate was flooded by the River Taff bursting it's banks. The Treasury for January 1961 records the incident;

> "Many families were evacuated from the Gabalfa estate, everything on ground level was flooded and ruined by water and filthy slime. The new Gabalfa Hall was offered to the civil authorities as a dormitory for residents and it has been gratefully used as headquarters for the WVS and Civil Defence. Beds and stores were packed into the hall.
> Sister Joyce and Sister Heulwen have worked with representatives of all churches to seek to alleviate the suffering of those affected by the floods." [45]

Initially, Sister Joyce had lodging in Ty Mawr Road, Llandaff, but was eventually given a flat on the estate in Gabalfa Avenue. [46]

Sister Joyce was in sole charge of the Gabalfa Hall and her weekly schedule was very demanding, as follows;

Sunday	10:30	Service
	2:45	Sunday School
	6:30	Service
Monday	6:00	Intermediate Christian Endeavour 11-14 years
Wednesday	6:00	Children Meeting
	7:30	Young Peoples Fellowship 14 + years
Thursday	2:45	Sisterhood
	7:30	Bible study and prayer [46]

Besides the heavy weekly workload, Sister Joyce was a well-known conference speaker and Sisterhood speaker.

In 1964, the IVF held a mission on the Gabalfa Estate, where students from Cardiff University, assisted by Sister Joyce, evangelised the area.

Maybe as a result of the 'groundwork' carried out during the mission, The Treasury March 1967 refers to a time of blessing at Gabalfa Hall as follows;

> "the breakthrough which happened towards the end of the year (1966) is being vigorously followed up. Nearly 100 young people came to a service and many came under conviction of sin. Ten of them finally decided and accepted the Lord Jesus Christ as their Saviour. They are going on well. They patrol the estate on 'fishing expeditions,' especially when the public house closes. They have been very successful and persuaded many who have never before entered a place of worship to come into church. We pray that what Gabalfa has experienced already ,may be the experience of every church and hall." [47]

Sister Joyce followed up this 'breakthrough' by a vigorous programme of summer camps as follows;

> "Christian work was carried on during August, as Sister Joyce Dowber this year again took teenagers to Summer Christian Camps.
>
> 1st Camp   July 29 – Aug 5 for seniors at Bryn Y Groes, Bala.
> 2nd Camp Aug 12 – Aug 19 Gabalfa Camp in the Youth Centre at Tresaith, Cardigan. Twenty-one adults and children attended. Each days programme included a religious service, a Bible study, as well as sea bathing, table tennis and beach games.
>
> The children and young people from the congested Gabalfa area greatly appreciated this visit to some of the loveliest beauty spots in Wales. Indeed some of them asked if they could start paying now for next year. We owe Sister Joyce a debt of gratitude for this very self-sacrificing work for the children under her care." [48]

However, it certainly wasn't easy for Sister Joyce, there was always opposition.

In 1967 there is a letter to J North, Builders asking for repairs to the church, including stronger doors to withstand hooliganism. [46]

Similarly, there is a letter to the Council in 1968 asking for the repair of the church boundary wall as the children are using the fallen bricks as missiles aimed at the church. [46]

After completing eight years of service at Gabalfa, Sister Joyce became a member of Heath Church. Sunday services then ceased in Gabalfa, although the Sunday School continued until 1971. Sister Joyce married Mr Richard Akrill in 1969 and both rendered many, many years of faithful service at Heath Church, Cardiff. [49]

Ringland Estate, Newport

This vast housing estate in Newport consisted mostly of housing and flats which were built by the local Council during the 1950s and 1960s. Many of the residents worked in the newly opened Llanwern Steelworks. In the Treasury November 1960, it is recorded that a young lady from Liverpool, Miss Joan Tolley, is studying at Ridgelands Bible College, with a view to becoming a Sister of the People. The Presbyterian Church on the Ringland Estate was opened on the 20th of November 1960 [50] and Sister Joan Tolley commenced as a Sister of the People on the Ringland Estate in summer/autumn 1961. [51]

It was not an easy placement as this estate was vast, the church was newly opened and there were all the problems an estate of this type presents.

Sister Joan Tolley worked exceptionally hard over almost three years, but resigned from the Forward Movement in 1964, when she married Rev John M Davies. They had a very fruitful ministry, initially in Port Tennant and the Burrows, Swansea and later in Clydach, then Maesteg and finally in Flint.

Courtesy of Sister Heulwen Jones (deceased)
Sisters of the People in the late 1950s

In the centre of the back row is Senior Sister Alison Jones, a product of Malpas Road Church, Newport. She trained at Star Hall Bible College, Manchester, has given over 50 years' service and founded her own mission at Grove Place, Morriston, where she started from scratch, won the people for Christ and built up a strong church.

On her left is Sister Mair Jones, bravely carrying on in the mining area of Markham in Monmouthshire. On her right is Sister Gwen Morrow who takes the church to the people on the great housing estate at Sandfields, Port Talbot, probably the largest in Wales, with a much bigger population than we find in many large towns.

In the front row on the left is Sister Kathleen Walker of Malpas Court, Newport – handicapped because there is no church building of any kind on that large housing estate of 16,000 people. There is a Sunday School of over 200 meeting in the council school and young peoples' meetings in the week and a sisterhood in a council house, by kind invitation of an elder of Malpas Road Church.

Second on the left in the front row is Sister Elsie Hole of East Moors, a colleague of the late Rev William Jones, of concertina fame, and she continues to carry on a great social redemptive work in that part of Cardiff.

Next to her in the front row is Sister Heulwen Jones of Kingsway Mission, who succeeded Sister Watkins, who laid the foundation of that Christian mission, situated in a back street of 200 homes where live 1,200 people, on the back door of our Welsh chapel.

On her right is Sister Margaret Hayes, a product of the Forward Movement – brought up at the Memorial Hall, Cardiff and working on the housing estate at Gorof, Swansea Valley, where the work is tougher now than it was in the old days of unspeakable poverty and slumdom that some of us remember.

Sisters Emily Roberts, Caernarvon, Ruby Rook, Caerphilly, Mary Williams, Trethomas and B E Williams, Wrexham were unavoidably absent when this photo was taken.

Brief Encounters

There are a few Sisters of the People who are mentioned briefly but little else has been recorded, and there are some Sisters who served for a brief period only, and there are others who offered for training but no other information has been found.

I have recorded them here for posterity:-

Mair Davies - (Treasury Nov 1947) - a young Sister from Liverpool has offered her service and has been joyfully accepted by the Forward Movement. Miss Mair Davies has been accepted as a student by the Faculty of Theology at Bangor University where she intends pursuing the Diploma Course in Theology. We hope the local church will be able to allow Miss Davies opportunities for acquiring experience in the more practical side of the work.

Ruth Parfitt - when the Rev Parfitt died in 1955, he was Minister at Jerusalem and Moorland Road, Cardiff. His wife Ruth was accepted as a Sister of the People to continue his ministry and work alongside Elsie Hole who had been a Sister of the People for many years at Jerusalem and Moorland Road.

Sister Ruth Parfitt subsequently married and stood down from the work. (Calvinistic Methodist Archive AZ31/410).

Mavis Lewis-Evans – (Treasury April 1955) – records that Miss Mavis Lewis-Evans from Welshpool has been accepted for training as a Sister of the People at the Ridgelands Bible College. In the Treasury September 1956, it is recorded that whilst she was training she worked in the holidays as a probationer at Trecenydd, Caerphilly.

In the Treasury March 1957 it is recorded that Sister Mavis Lewis-Evans had finished her training and had been placed at Kingsway Hall, Cardiff to replace Sister Watkins, who was retiring.

In the Treasury June 1957 it is recorded that Sister Mavis Lewis-Evans had resigned her role as Sister of the People.

Sister Ruby Rook – (Treasury March 1957) – records the appointment of a new Sister of the People. Ruby Rook SRN of Bristol, trained at Redlands College and after completing her training she worked with Miss Gladys Alywood amongst the Chinese in London. She is now placed as a Sister of the People at Trecenydd, Caerphilly.

Elizabeth Ann Davies – From Swansea offered for training as a Sister of the People (Treasury Aug 1963)

Priscilla Mary John – From Solva, Pembrokeshire offered for training as a Sister of the People (Treasury Aug 1963)

Jean E Davies SRN – From Cardiff accepted for training at Carey Hall United Missionary College, Selly Oak, Birmingham for training as a Sister of the People. She had previously given voluntary service at Kingsway, Cardiff and latterly Gabalfa, Cardiff (Treasury Oct 1963).

After completing training in October 1965, Sister Jean Davies commenced work in Hengwrt, Briton Ferry. A new hall had opened there on the 30th of April 1964 (Treasury Oct 1965) at the end of 1965 Sister Davies resigned from the Forward Movement and subsequently she married Mr A Vick (Treasury Jan 1966).

<><><><><><>

Chapter Eleven – Warts and All

The work of the Sisters of the People was certainly challenging in many ways. They were absolutely dedicated and selfless in their service. They had the hardest of work amongst the hardest of people in the hardest of circumstances.

Before the introduction of the Welfare State, which was brought in immediately after World War Two, the Sisters of the People dealt with abject poverty, gross immorality and rampant drunkenness and all the effects it has on people, families and communities. Remembering that the Sisters of the People came from good, sheltered, protective Christian homes. Even with the training they received nothing quite prepared them for what they were called upon to deal with. Yet compelled by the love of Christ and in the power of the Holy Spirit they persevered. In the report of the Women's Branch in 1906, it states;

> "Few have any idea of the burden of souls which our Sisters feel as they go from house to house, from street to street, where sin and misery are rampant. They greatly need our prayers" [1]

Similarly in the Torch, in 1906 it states;

> "The poverty which our Sisters meet with everywhere at this time is terrible. It baffles them at every point and throws them back on their own resources. They are not in a position to materially help, and how can they speak to those about their souls whose bodies are starving and near naked." [2]

In the Annual Report of the Women's Branch in 1909 it states;

> "Having received thorough Bible training and insight into nursing, our Sisters do all in their power to minister to soul and body diseased. Frequently, they are the means of bringing unity, comfort, and everything that constitutes homelife to those who, through their own sin or misfortune, have lost or destroyed their homes, and many have either in their own homes sought the Lord and found Him or been induced by the importunate pleadings of our Sisters to attend our Halls, and there

have found the Saviour" In the results of their work is verified the saying that while a man sets about his work of cleaning with a broom, a women does it with her tears. He leaves it clean she leaves it also comforted". [3]

John Pugh's vision for a local Training Institute was never realised, but the Sisters of the People were all trained at various Theological and Missionary Training Institutes across the UK and further abroad. This however meant that there was no uniform standard for the training the Sisters received, neither was it specific to the roles they undertook. Training Institutes attended by the Sister's of the People included, Bible Training School, Manchester, Bible Training School, Liverpool, South Wales Bible Training Institute, Redlands College, London, Ridgelands College, Kent, Carey Hall United Mission College, Selly Oak, Faculty of Theology, Bangor University, and as far afield as the Bible Institute in Los Angeles (a sister Institute to the Moody Bible Institute)

It is regularly recorded, particularly in the 1950s and 1960s that a Sister had experienced a breakdown and was prescribed a month's rest.

The Calvinistic Methodist archive at the National Library of Wales records the serious effect on one Sister's mental health where it is recorded;

> "She is very depressed and anxious and asked me to give in her resignation. She is a person of great moral commitment and she has worked quite selflessly at her work. The decision has involved not only her sense of personal failure that she was unable to meet demands made upon her, but also of vocational failure and an acute sense of having proved unworthy of her church and Christian principles, despite a strong urge to do so." [4]

Sisters were often 'lone workers' sometimes in sole charge of Forward Movement halls and they had to do everything. In the Torch in 1908 the Women's Branch state;

> "Sisters are working alone amidst the most sordid surroundings; they pine for fellowship and sympathy. An occasional reunion would be a great help to them all, if only some good friend would make it possible

by meeting their travelling expenses, which would not amount to much."[4a]

They were often accommodated in council or rented accommodation in the areas where they worked, so in that sense they were 'always on the job' and always on call. Those Sisters who were attached to Halls where there was a Minister, and to whom they were accountable, often experienced some difficulties. The Sisters were undoubtedly "Gospel ladies " and as liberal theology made steady inroads into the churches of the denomination, this was a great discouragement for some Sisters of the People working alongside liberal Ministers.

Looking at the archives and journals at that time, many of the Sisters were constantly moved to wherever the greatest need was, and sometimes to cover in the absence of a Minister. This didn't really make for a 'settled ministry,' as they had to start from scratch all over again in building up relationships with the people in the community outside of the church. Some Sisters were 'long serving' with thirty or forty or even fifty years service. Others found husbands, often within the denomination and only served for a few years. Others were widows of Ministers and they continued their husbands' ministries as Sisters of the People.

The pay for the Sisters of the People was always meagre and placed them at subsistence level. When the first Sister was appointed in 1903, the salary was £52 per year. [5] By 1921 it had risen to £150 per year [6] and by 1957 it had risen to £300 per year. [7]

The Forward Movement had incurred a large debt resulting from the building of a large number of halls in the first 20 years of its ministry. Against this background, the Women's Branch were tasked with raising the funds to support both the Sisters of the People and the Kingswood Treborth Home, so a very large proportion of the financial support came from the women of the denomination. There was always a much greater need for the work of the Sisters of the People than there was money available to develop the work. There were often times when the Women's Branch were devoid of money and urgent appeals were sent out. At their greatest in number, the Sisters of the People numbered no more than about 12. Also, particularly in the early years of the work of the Sisters of the People, when roles were being defined and established, the attitude to women, at that time, could be very unhelpful.

In 1907 the Secretary of the Women's Branch, writes as follows;

> "We deplore the continued feeble health of our beloved Superintendent (Rev John Pugh). As women workers in the service of the King, we cannot speak too highly of one who has always set a high value upon the work of women, who has always encouraged them to use their talents and gifts in the highest cause and has been unsparing in his praise of their efforts. Would that all servants of God were equally generous in their treatment of their Sisters in the work." [8]

Also, in 1907, Mrs Tydfil Thomas, Secretary of the Women's Branch in a eulogy to Rev John Pugh writes;

> "To him it was easier to praise than to blame, and on that account he made us do and give our best in the work. It is this that, coupled with a true spirit of chivalry towards women, which has assured us women a place in the great work of the Forward Movement. Dr Pugh had an extraordinarily high opinion of the power of women in the establishment of Christ's Kingdom on earth." [9]

Whilst the Sisters of the People did outstanding work, there were some anomalies to their ministry. One of these was highlighted by Sister Kate Thomas, who was at Trethomas for many years and served as a Sister of the People for 44 years. Whilst she was in charge of the Forward Movement Hall at Hereford during World War One, she was accepted as a woman preacher by the Radnor and Brecon Presbytery. When she moved back to Trethomas, she was given a letter to transfer to the Glamorgan Presbytery East and her name entered into the Concessional Diary as a preacher.

For some time at Trethomas, apart from the Vicar of the parish, she was the only minister. Her services were so highly appreciated that the church at Trethomas brought to the Presbytery, a request for her ordination. But it was not to be accepted. But here is one instance of Sister Kate's ministerial handicap. In one report from Sister Kate on her work, she states that a mother had asked her to baptise her very sick baby, but she could not. The doctor attended the sick baby and stated that the baby was dying and needed to be baptised. The mother responded that she had asked Sister Kate to baptise her baby, but Sister Kate was unable to do so. So the doctor baptised the baby and the baby died. The doctor was a Roman Catholic. Sister Kate says that this happens very often – the doctor baptises them and she buries them. [10]

It was before, and certainly after the decision by the Presbyterian Church of Wales to admit women as ordained ministers (1978), that the role for Sisters of the People declined. The "glory days" for the Sisters of the People were beginning to wane. In 1968 a Mission Board was formed uniting the Overseas Mission and the Forward Movement. A joint committee was set up representing both works. All rallies were united with speakers representing both works. The Mission Board also became responsible for the salaries of the Sisters of the People (instead of the Women's Branch). [10a]

The Treasury in 1968 records;

> "We have had no applications from men or women for service with the Forward Movement for a long time." [11]

Thus, unfortunately it marked the beginning of the end and the last remaining Sister of the People, Heulwen Jones of the Kingsway Hall, Cardiff retired in 1993, when the Hall was closed.

However, Heulwen Jones had been ordained sometime after 1978 (when the first women were admitted) as she bore the title 'Reverend'.

Thus as one chapter closed for the ministry of women, yet another chapter opened in the form of ordination of women to the ministry of the church.

<><><><><><>

Chapter Twelve – Long Serving Sisters of the People

Here are the mini testimonies of 7 long serving Sisters of the People, who between them gave a collective total of 251 years service to the Forward Movement. It is so fitting that an attempt is made in this book to record and honour their faithful service and the service of all the Sisters of the People, whose legacy, to date, has been unrecorded.

Sister Alison Jones

Sister Alison Jones, Morriston (Grove Place) died 30th April 1960 after 55 years' service as a Sister of the People, (42 years at Morriston). She previously ministered at Port Tennant, Swansea, Merthyr Tydfil and Grangetown, Cardiff. The following appreciation of the work of Sister Alison after 50 years' service appeared in the Treasury in 1957 as follows. Sister Alison Jones was born in Magill, Adelaide, South Australia and when at the age of seven she lost her mother, her father decided to return to his native land bringing his family with him. Brought up in the Anglican Communion as a young girl, Alison was invited to attend church at Malpas Road, Newport and there as she aptly put it, she was "born again" and with that experience came a deep, deep longing to serve her Saviour. She soon found an opportunity for doing so by offering herself as a Sister of the People. She was conscious of her youth and felt so young and feeling that youthful looks might in some manner detract from her work, she thought she might add years to herself by dressing to look much older than she really was. But Dr John Pugh must have detected something of this for when she went to see him he asked her, "how old are you?" He assured her that what mattered most in the service of Christ were grace and common sense. He asked her, "is there much starch in you? For if so you will soon loose it in the work of the Forward Movement."

She was initiated into the work at Grangetown Hall, Cardiff, working in conjunction with Rev Howell Harris Hughes. After a while Sister Alison asked to be released of her duties in order to attend a Training college. This was granted her on condition that she returned to the Forward Movement. She went to the Bible Training School, Manchester. When she returned to Wales, she was sent to Merthyr Tydfil and worked with Rev B G Barker, known as Sargent Barker, a wonderful man of God who later left for Dr Odell's Mission on the Ohio River. Later on she was sent to the Burrows and Port Tennant Road, Swansea, where she worked with Rev William Meredith. This was no easy place to labour. The Burrows then was a tin shed, but now there is a fine building erected on the site. It was from here that Sister Alison was sent to Grove Place and Central Hall, Morriston and it is largely with Morriston that her name is associated in the minds of many. Grove Place itself was like The Burrows, only a tin shed in those days. By today, it too had been transformed into a beautiful building. Rev William Jones was minister, known in his day far and wide as an Evangelist. Here at Grove Place, Sister Alison had been in full charge for many years and has seen the birth of many souls. She has seen many changes in the course of the years, not only has the whole district completely changed, but miserable homes have been made happy and brands have been snatched from the burning.

She continues her work and is as enthusiastic as ever. Her service is as great and as happy now as it was when she first came, for she has a very keen awareness of the presence of her Lord and Master, who has helped her through many difficulties and hardships.

She is a Sister greatly beloved, her kindness, her quiet, unobtrusive manner are clearly discerned at all times. It has been a privilege and a pleasure to have known her for does not the light and the joy of the Gospel radiate from her. She is well known not only in Morriston, but in the whole of the Swansea area and in the Glamorgan Presbytery West as the handmaid of the Lord. Fifty years' service is a wonderful record. It is a record of which one may be proud, yet sister Alison is very humble concerning this long service and is grateful to God for having had the opportunity for so long of being in the highest and most rewarding service in the world. What a long chapter it has been. She has served the Forward Movement from the time of Dr John Pugh and thus has worked under four Superintendents.

May she long be spared to continue with the work which is so dear to her heart and to obey the injunction of Christ, "in as much as ye have done it unto one of the least of these, my brethren, ye have done it unto me." [1]

Sister Kate Jones

In memoriam Catherine Mary Jones (Sister Kate) Benllech, Anglesey

Catherine Mary Jones was born in Bryn Tawel, Bangor in 1883. She was nurtured in the church at Benea and she received an overwhelming and lasting Pentecost of the Holy Spirit in the revival of 1904/05. Her rich experience of the salvation which is in Christ Jesus compelled her to give her life in His service. She commenced to preach in 1907 and in 1912, she was accepted to the noble band of Sister of the People under the supervision of the Forward Movement. She served at Central Hall, Swansea and Gorse, Cwmbala and at Hereford and for 32 years at Trethomas and Trecynydd. She also assisted the Rev John Thomas in his work as secretary of the Forward Movement. She retired, if retirement is the appropriate word, in 1956, having laboured diligently as a Sister of the People for 44 years, but her labouring did not cease. Rather she continued to preach the Word up to her 90th birthday and witnessed to the end being loved and respected by all. She died 24th of September 1977 aged 94 years. [2]

Sister Elsie Hole

Sister Elsie Hole started as a Sister of the People in 1926, based at Eastmoors Hall, Splott, Cardiff, which was the first Forward Movement Hall to be opened. Because of the areas in which she worked; she was often referred to as a 'Slum Sister.'

Sister Elsie was active along with Rev W Jones in setting up the Splott Institute. The Eastmoor Hall was refurbished to meet the recreational needs of the youth of the area as an attempt to reach and influence them with the Gospel. This was almost a revolutionary idea at the time. Worshippers at Eastmoors Hall transferred to Jerusalem. Thus sister Elsie spent her time working between the three centres – Eastmoors, Jerusalem and Moorland Road Hall.

Sister Elsie retired in 1966 after 40 years' service. [3]

The Treasury in December 1966 records that sister Elsie was provided with a large celebration to recognise her 40 years' service and her retirement. [4]

Sister Esther Francis

The Treasury in 1943 records a eulogy for Sister Esther as follows:;

"Sister Esther Eliza Francis was of English stock, cradled in the Evangelical faith and devoted herself to home mission work for the past 30 years. She served as a Sister of the People in the Forward Movement at The Burrows, Swansea, until weakness and the care of her beloved mother broke the continuity of her service. On her mother's decease, she renewed her service in our church in pioneer visitation at Mynachdy, Cardiff and in ministry at Trecenydd, Caerphilly and Kingsway, Cardiff, in happy association with those in charge of these centres.

She was a beautiful, radiant messenger of the faith and joy of the Gospel. Her saintly witness was of the lily work on the pillars of God's house and her influence filled the sanctuary as the perfume from an alabaster box of ointment. Many will call her ministry a blessing, unfailing in it's great strength. Her mortal remains were buried as she desired amongst, 'the common people' whom she loved and served latterly at Trecenydd. They were accompanied to their last resting place amid every mark of respect, esteem and triumph over death after a service held at the Mission Centre of Trecynydd Church, over which the beloved pastor, the Rev Watcyn M Price resided. [5]

Sister Watkins

Work for Christ – an article that appeared in the Treasury in May 1954, written by Sister Watkins and reflecting upon her 28 years' service as a Sister of the People as she anticipated retirement;

"I had the essential experience when a child of 12 of a deep conviction of sin, and a personal knowledge of a living Saviour, accompanied by deep joy and love for Christ. The experience is ever like a newly minted coin – it has never lost its lustre. There was borne into my heart a great desire to work for Christ. Through reading, I learned that there were multitudes of poor people and children that never had a chance in life. I longed to help them. It was clearly a vision of need and a call, the accomplishment of which was humanly impossible. I did not know how to find such people and had no qualifications for the work, nor the means to be qualified. This love for Christ and a deep yearning of the soul to serve Him was in a very poor earthen vessel.

However, there is nothing impossible with God. He led me by a strange way into a strange land, and through the hard school of fighting one's way, and after some years of much travelling and varied experiences, I came to where two ways opened for me. I had just enough money to return to my beloved Wales, which was very tempting, or to apply for an entrance into the Bible Institute of Los Angeles, California (sister Institute to the Moody Institute at Chicago), to qualify as a worker for Christ. It was a time of deep soul searching, of great abandonment of all for Christ. I was accepted as a student into the Bible Institute. This meant a choice opportunity to be taught by able men of God, the best known in this country being the Dean of the Institute, the Rev Dr R A Torrey. The practical side of the training gave insight and knowledge of human nature through extensive visitation of hospitals and prisons, and great experience of 'rightly dividing' the word of God was gained by practising personal Evangelism.

We were given a worldwide vision of the Kingdom through hearing missionaries from every land speaking of their work and it's needs. I was greatly influenced by the China Inland Mission speakers. The way was opened for me to go to this needy field at the close of my studies at the Bible Institute, but it was not to be. That was not the place of God's appointment for me. I came back to Wales and that in itself is proof that God did not want my little sum of money but obedience, for after two years of heavy expenses, I still had enough money to pay my fare home and a little over – 'bread enough and to spare.'

During the years at the Bible Institute, I often received money, but never knew the giver or the givers. Sometimes it was pushed under the door of my room, other times I found sums of money in my letterbox. But one day I found a much larger sum than usual and I felt that I must make it my business to search for the giver. I went to one whom I thought the most likely to be doing this After telling my story I was simply asked who was the 'giver of all good gifts' and was told to thank Him. That put an end to all my enquiries and I just lifted up my heart in thanks to God and

I have reason to continue to be thankful ever since. God asks for our all, in order that it may come to us again in abounding blessings.

In 1926 the Forward Movement, the name given to the Home Mission branch of the Presbyterian Church in Wales, accepted me as a worker at the Kingswood Treborth Home. This was a preventative work among young girls and the opening proved to be the leading to my life's work.

The Superintendent of the Forward Movement entrusted me with one of their small Halls placed in a poor and populous district of the City of Cardiff. I am very thankful to them for this favour, for it brought me to the people and children of my vision. Here I was at last, in the midst of that multitude. I have found that reality is sterner than vision and I have needed all the lessons that I have learned since the day of vision in order to translate it into service. I was now in another school – that of learning the true state of the people in the district. I shall never forget being overwhelmed with sight of poverty in property and people and homes with tales of want and woe, and with hardness of spirit. They were in truth the depressing Parish Relief and Dole days. I could give very little material help, but even if I had great sums of money that would have made very little impression on such a vast want among so many.

I learned that one factor in human life is the cause of much poverty and ailments of the body and mind. If the State could deal with that, it would indeed be a Welfare State. The fact is sin, and there is only one remedy. The church possess it, and it is her responsibility to make it possible for the remedy to reach all for whom Christ died. The Gospel of God is that remedy. This is what the Forward Movement seeks to do, and this is how they do it.

First of all, if at all possible, they secure a hall which they call a Centre, a meeting place in the midst of the people. Then they spread the wings of counsel and care over the whole of the neighbourhood. They place in the neighbourhood an Evangelist or a Sister of the People, to take the Gospel to the homes of the people. The worker so placed, will first of all seek to win the confidence of the people, through visiting them, and through seeking to know their circumstances and then knowing the groove of their minds.

The worker will teach the Word of God, backed by example and personal witness. The Forward Movement Centre that I came to was called the Fitzroy Street Mission. It was an unadorned little room that had once

been a stable. There awaiting to welcome me was a handful of young people. They were the legacy of the Plasnewydd Presbyterian Church, which had undertaken the responsibility of the work some years previously. They did a great work, the fruit of which still remains.
But the burden had become too heavy for the church and the Forward Movement took over the work. The handful of you remained however and were of the greatest blessing to me then and through the succeeding years. Through their ministry I was introduced to people and homes that gave me a good start.
The Crwys Hall Church next became our mother church. Within a year, the Forward Movement had bought a Mission Hall in the same neighbourhood which was more suitable for the work." [6]

The oversight of Crwys Hall Church ended in September 1949. A meeting was held at the new Kingsway Hall and it was incorporated into the Presbyterian Church of Wales under the jurisdiction of the Forward Movement. Sister Watkins worked tirelessly at the Kingsway Hall until she indicated in 1954 that she wished to retire, which she did. However, it was difficult to find a replacement Sister of the People, so Sister Watkins returned from retirement to cover the Kingsway Hall until a replacement Sister could be appointed.

Eventually, Sister Heulwen Jones was appointed on the 1st of September 1957 as the new Sister of the People at Kingsway Hall.

Sister Heulwen Jones

Sister Heulwen Jones was from Llanelli and applied to the Forward Movement to become a Sister of the People in 1955. She trained at Ridgelands College in Kent for two years and after completing training was appointed as a Sister of the People at Kingsway Hall, Cardiff. She started on the 1st of September 1957 and when the new Forward Movement Hall opened on the Gabalfa Estate in Cardiff on the 6th of December 1959, Sister Heulwen covered Gabalfa on a temporary basis as well as Kingsway Hall, assisted by a band of workers drawn from Heath Church.

Other than the episode of cover at Gabalfa, Sister Heulwen was based at Kingsway, in sole charge for 36 years.

Reporting in the Treasury November 1980 she writes as follows;

"geographically, the Kingsway Hall is situated at a lower level than the main thoroughfare of Crwys Road, with two dozen steps descending to the church building, which is on the corner of Rhymney and Harriet Streets, Cathays, Cardiff. Socially, this area is working class and racially it is heavily mixed with children from South Africa, Sri Lanka, West Indies, Malta and Portugal, having passed through the Sunday School. Religiously, the children come from nominally Christian homes and the church is usually packed out for annual Carol service and Children's Prize Giving Services.

The church served a thickly populated area around Rhymney and Harriett Streets. Such is the diversity of the population of this area, that these streets alone have 1,200 adults on the electoral roll and a minimum speculated figure of 2,500 children. I say 'minimum' because one section of Rhymney Street houses large families of six to nine children. Rhymney street is one long row of 200 terraced houses., It is another 'Coronation Street', with no front garden, latch-key children and with the main Rhondda railway line running at the back of its pocket handkerchief backyard. With no recreation centre in the locality, not even a play corner for the infants, the children are compelled either to watch TV, or play in the heavily traffic-flowing streets. In the hot, sticky, summer weather, the elderly and infirm, sit on chairs parked on pavements outside their front doors. In the wet, drizzly, foggy weather of winter months, the sight is dismal as the street is bare and empty, coloured only by the lit up electric lampstands.

Is there any wonder that an eight-year-old boy actually kicked down the back door of the church with a view to drawing attention to himself?

Is there any wonder that a 13-year-old ran to the church for refuge after absconding from an Assessment Centre, where he had been sent for stealing motorcycles. Is there any wonder that the bright and intelligent leave the area for a socially and environmentally improved area. The church has its own trophies of grace. The records reveal a list of outstanding deathbed conversions among the elderly. One a chronic alcoholic. An amazing physical miracle on a 12-year-old girl is still talked about, together with a mental transformation on a crippled lady steeped in spiritualism, the full recovery of a schizophrenic youth mentally broken down because of drug addiction and now engaged in missionary work in the Middle East, the liberation of many from spiritual condemnation, and the re-direction of many into useful citizens in the community.

My aim is to have a properly equipped 'Teen Challenge Centre,' where the children and youth can come and enjoy Christian films, coffee, music, guitar groups etc. The Sunday School register at present shows over 70 children and many of these are ready for youth work. My aim is to have a properly equipped 'Counsel Chamber' where the emotionally distressed and physically troubled can come for prayer, guidance, comfort and help. My aim is to have a properly equipped 'Saturday Bible School' to meet the needs of the physically sick, mentally distressed and the spiritually hungry people. The church building built in 1887, seats 150 and previous efforts of an 'Open Saturday' has shown the need and response to such a project.

My aim is to have a structurally safe and pleasant 'centre' to match the improvements made of many of these 100-year-old terraced houses and so preach the gospel to both coloured and white, young and old, in their own area.

My aim is to meet the particular cry of the 'Early Teen Youth' when they rightly and continually cry, 'we have nothing to do, we have nowhere to go.'[7]

Sister Heulwen was ordained when eventually women were accepted as ministers by the Presbyterian Church of Wales and she became Rev Heulwen Jones.

She served almost exclusively at Kingsway Hall but was also a noted conference speaker and Sisterhood speaker.

The church became very much reduced in numbers and the Kingsway Hall closed on the 20th of April 1993, thus ending the service of Heulwen Jones after 36 years of faithful, fruitful ministry. She was the last serving Sister of the People.

Sister Margaret Jones

Sister Margaret Jones commenced work at Caernarvon in 1919. She then came to South Wales and founded the Gorse Mission Hall in Cwmbwrla, which opened in 1926. Sister Jones ministered at Gorse Mission Hall for 21 years.

Subsequently, she ministered at Ely, Cardiff, Pontnewydd, Mon. She retired in 1947 due to ill health. The Treasury February 1946 records the following tribute;

> "She has served the Forward Movement for over a quarter of a century, with varying experiences of difficulty and joy which mission work entails. We thank our dear sister for her excellent work and valiant spirit and pray that with the return of strength after anxious war years with the blackout and the blitz placing her life in peril, she may be allowed of God to renew the joy of His salvation in further service." [8]

Sadly, Sister Margaret Jones died in 1949. [9]

<><><><><><>

Chapter Thirteen – Champions of The Cause

The work of the Sisters of the People and the work of Kingswood- Treborth Rescue and Prevention Home, would have been impossible without the staunch support and clear direction and leading of the officers of the Women's Branch of the Forward Movement, under whose control the work came. The officers of the Women's Branch gave such incalculable service to the Forward Movement as cannot possibly be recorded in a way that it deserves.

Mrs Tydfil Thomas BA – Honorary Organising Secretary

A hard part of the burden and responsibility was borne by Mrs Tydfil E Thomas BA, who most efficiently filled the office of Organising Secretary of the Women's Branch (social Wing), together with that of Kingswood Treborth Home from August 1904 until 1937. In addition to the general work of Secretaryship, visiting the local branches and addressing Forward Movement Conferences, she kept the women's work forcibly before the churches of the denomination by her direct and well-informed articles which appeared month by month, with unbroken regularity in the Forward Movement Magazine the Torch.

Mrs Tydfil Thomas was recognised as a Welsh Evangelical pioneer in social work. She was the wife of Rev John Thomas, who was assistant to John Pugh and then General Secretary of the Forward Movement for many years. [1]

Mrs Dr J Saunders (Sara Maria Saunders) Honorary Treasurer

The First Treasurer of the Women's Branch of the Forward Movement was Mrs Sara Saunders. She was a prolific fundraiser to support the work of the Sisters of the People and the Rescue and Prevention Home. It is recorded in The Torch June 1908 that Mrs Saunders collected £750 (£112,000 at today's value) to match Mr John Cory's offer of £250.

Mrs Saunders was certainly a leader amongst women. The monthly Treasury records;

> "in 1908 a permanent women's refuge was established for the Forward Movement in Cardiff, mainly through the efforts of some of the women of our movement led by Mrs Saunders, we decided to purchase more commodious premises at Kingswood, Canton, Cardiff, where we might carry on rescue as well as prevention work." [2]

Mrs Saunders was a staunch supporter of the rescue work amongst disadvantaged women. She had a special interest in the destiny of girls and women , an awareness of the difficulties they faced and her faith in their potential, through the transforming power of the Gospel. Besides the tremendous energy she put into her role as treasurer of the Women's Branch, she also worked with the women's activities of the Abuse Movement (Symudiad Ymosodol), speaking at meetings, promoting the movement and helping with organising and fundraising.

Sara was married to the Rev John Saunders, they were a key couple in the early days of the Forward Movement, as well as during the 1904/05 revival in which both were deeply and significancy involved.

Mrs Dr J Pugh – President of the Women's Branch

Mrs Mary Pugh was the first President of the women's Branch of the Forward Movement, she was the wife of Rev John Pugh, Founder and Superintendent of the Forward Movement. She worked tirelessly to promote and support the work of the Women's Branch over many years.

Her daughter describes her thus;

> "My mother was a woman of intellectual ability and a suitable partner for a man of my father's capabilities. She was a strong character, a woman of personality and considerably bravery. She was an influential person, but her forcefulness was tempered by a great kindness and a warm heart." [3]

In The Torch 1907, in a tribute to the late Rev John Pugh, Mrs Tydfil Thomas, Secretary of the Women's Branch writes as follows in reference to Mrs Pugh;

> "And what shall we say to Mrs Pugh who was his inspiration, his true help meet, who with him nobly faced the storms and difficult places, was with

him in weakness and who's heart now yearns for him – his dear wife and our beloved President." [4]

In 1931, it was the 40th Anniversary of the formation of the Forward Movement and there were great celebrations. The Superintendent of the Forward Movement writes as follows;

> "letter from Mrs Dr Pugh on the 40th Anniversary of the Forward Movement: In view of the approaching celebration, we all unite in praising God for the gift of the 'elect lady', He gave Rev John Pugh equal to him in spirit, sacrifice and service. We thank God for sparing her to see this year and pray that as she surveys 'these 40 years' the Lord will fill her soul with refreshing from on high. Here is part of a letter she sent to my wife, after opening with greetings she says:
>> "it is just 55 years ago (how the years roll by) since I first had the joy of hearing the late Mrs Catherine Booth, the mother of the Salvation Army slum work and devoted wife of the late William Booth, the Founder of the Salvation Army. It was a drawing room meeting, and I shall never forget the earnestness and enthusiasm. It was the day of small things then – but she had a clear vision of the great work God would do through consecrated women in the slums. By today the whole world knows that a little has become a thousand." [5]

Mrs Pugh was making a direct comparison with how the work of the Forward Movement had flourished over 40 years, where it started in a tent in Eastmoors, Cardiff, to the vast number there are now of halls and churches throughout Wales.

Richard Burgess writes as follows;

> "Mrs Dr Pugh was and is as great a treasure as her husband. But for their devotion, her quiet ways, her patience, her sweetness of manner and her capability, Dr Pugh could not have borne the load from their first pastoral charge in Tredegar, to the hour of his return home to God. And, to our delight, Mrs Pugh is still with us as keen and unselfish as ever." [5]

Mrs Pugh died two years after the 40th Anniversary in 1933 aged 84. What a huge loss it was for the Women's Branch and the Forward Movement.

Ceridwen Peris (Mrs Alice Gray Jones) Organising Secretary, North Wales

Ceridwen Peris (pseudonym) was widely acknowledged for her long service to good causes and was awarded an OBE in 1921. She was a headmistress, writer, journal editor and temperance leader. She was the Organising Secretary of the North Wales Women's Branch of the Forward Movement.

She was a prolific fundraiser by her very effective deputation work., She was often accompanied by a Sister of the People, often Sister Lloyd, on grand tours of North Wales, raising the profile of the work of the Women's Branch and raising funds for the continuation of the work. The Women's Branch owe a debt of gratitude to Ceridwen Peris. She died in 1943 and was sadly missed by The Women's Branch.

Mrs Annie Pugh-Williams – Official Organiser of the Women's Work/Sisters of the People of the Home Mission

Mrs Annie Pugh-Williams was the daughter of the Rev John Pugh. Very early in her life she became her father's unpaid secretary and assistant, so the Forward Movement was in her blood. She married the Rev Watkin Williams and they laboured at Central Hall, Swansea. It was at that time that she felt the call to dedicate her life to the women of Wales and to this vision she was faithful to the end of her life.

In the days of industrial depression in South Wales, she gathered together a sisterhood numbering 700 at Central Hall – every women being wife, mother or sister of unemployed men. The motto of the sisterhood was 'every women my sister – all one in Christ Jesus.' Her vision soon overstepped the limits of one church and one town and in 1929 she formed The Swansea Free Church Women's Council which expanded into the West Wales Federation of Free Church Women's Council. She founded the Federation in 1943.

The value of her work and leadership was recognised across the border and in 1944, she was honoured with the presidency of the National Free Church Women's Council – the highest honour which can be conferred on a Free Church woman.

She always had a lively interest in the Forward Movement and she dedicated the last 20 years of her life entirely to the Forward Movement.

She was appointed official organiser of the Women's work, including responsibility for the Sisters of the People. She threw herself body and soul into the work. She established Home Mission Auxiliaries in every presbytery in North and South Wales and their growing effectiveness was due to her personal influence and unflagging zeal. She travelled hundreds of miles each year, visiting and encouraging the workers. She was a strange mixture of boldness and modesty. She feared neither criticism nor attack. Once she has set her mind on accomplishing her objective, she pursued it with untiring energy and courage. She wrote hundreds of letters and many will miss her letters, written in a characteristic hand, gracious and to the point. She was an outstanding public speaker, but she preferred to remain silent in the background. But over and above her talents was that strong, charming personality. She was beloved by the women of the denomination. She worked and wrote and travelled to the very end – debonair and optimistic. [5a]

(Extract from In Memoriam written by Rev Ieuan Phillips, Superintendent, Forward Movement)

Besides the incalculable service and support of the Women's Branch to the work of the Sisters of the People and the Kingswood – Treborth Home, it is important to recognise the systematic, sacrificial giving of the members of the denomination to support the work.

Each gave according to their means. It also seems right however, to recognise the vast generosity of the Davies family and the Cory family to the work of the Women's Branch, which sustained it over many years.

The Davies Family of Llandinam

David Davies (1818 – 1890)

David Davies was a self-made man, he built railways, owned a number of collieries and was most noted for building Barry Dock.

The Christian Standard November 1892 records;

"he never won a victory in business without consecrating a large portion of his spoils to the service of religion. He married Miss Margaret Jones, and like her husband the leading feature in Mrs Davies' character was the generous spirit she showed towards The Lord's cause. This she possessed before she knew Mr Davies, and this continues to sway her powerfully. Though the generous spirit was strong in Mr Davies, it would be impossible for him to continue to give in such a princely manner to such a number of objects, were it not for the strong and warm encouragement he received at home. They formed themselves into a deep and wide river of generosity that was admired by all." [6]

The Forward Movement Hall in Cowbridge Road, Canton, Cardiff was named the David Davies Memorial Hall when it opened in 1893, as a lasting memory to the beneficence of Mr David Davies.

Edward Davies (1852 – 1898)

Edward Davies was the only son of David Davies and Edward took over the business upon the death of his father. Edward Davies of Llandinam was undoubtedly the Forward Movement's greatest financial supporter, a man of great wealth but one who regarded himself as a steward of that wealth. Many people were convinced that but for the generous support of Edward Davies, the Forward Movement would have collapsed in its early youth.

Edward Davies generously contributed towards the work because he was devout, spiritually minded and deeply concerned about the salvation of the great masses of people in cities, towns and industrial areas. He was an active missionary, taking a good share in the great work done by his intelligent and sympathetic interest and his great monetary contributions. [7] Edward Davies was the Treasurer of the Forward Movement and his death on the 1st of January 1898 at the early age of 45 was a great loss for the Forward Movement.

Gwendoline and Margaret Davies

Edward Davies had three children, David, Gwendoline and Margaret. Just as remarkable as Edward Davies was in his financial support of the work, his two daughters Gwendoline and Margaret were earnest Calvinistic Methodist women. They inherited much of their grandfather's wealth, but also his strongly developed sense of social responsibility. They were steadfast church goers, Sabbatarians and lifelong teetotallers. Along with their mother, Mrs Edward Davies, who was President of the Women's Branch at one time, they were staunch supporters of the Women's Branch with their many very generous donations.

John and Richard Cory

John Cory   (1828 – 1910)
Richard Cory   (1830 – 1914)

Their business was known as Cory Brothers, based in Cardiff. They were shipping and coal magnets with worldwide business interests. The family were deeply religious and morning prayers were said daily at Cory Brothers' offices.

John and Richard Cory were very generous philanthropists, they gave abundantly to the Women's Branch of the Forward Movement, but also to many other faith-based enterprises.

It is impossible to know the full extent of the spiritual work wrought, the number of souls saved, the hungry fed and the naked clothed through the vast and generous sums of money given in support of the Sisters of the People and the Kingswood-Treborth Home.

However A W Tozer sums up it's worth beautifully. He says:

"As base a thing as money often is, yet it can be transmuted into everlasting treasure. It can be converted into food for the hungry and clothing for the poor. It can keep a missionary actively winning the lost to the light of the Gospel and thus transmute itself into heavenly values. Any temporal possession can be turned into everlasting wealth. Whatever is given to Christ is immediately touched with immortality" [8]

<><><><><><>

Chapter Fourteen – What Shall We Say to These Things?

It is recalled that Rev William Ross of Cowcaddens, Glasgow, a dear friend and mentor of Rev John Pugh, had spoken one day to a poor lady about her soul, who looking pathetically in his face had replied;

> Oh Mr Ross, if you were as hungry as I am, you wouldn't have time to think about your soul."

That woman's face and answer left such a profound impression on Rev Ross' tender nature that was never to go away. He was deeply challenged and remembered the Lord's attitude to such people; 'when He saw the multitude He had compassion on them.' [1]

So, should social engagement be the concern of the churches not because of direct religiously inspired condemnation of injustices, but because environmental conditions hinder the church's spiritual mission (as in the example above).

"Men and women have bodies to be fed as well as souls to be saved. And empty cupboards are not unrelated to empty churches." [2]

The Sisters of the People over the 90 years that such ministries were in place, showed unequivocally the compassion and love of Christ to the poverty stricken, the immoral, the fallen, the drunkards, the fatherless, the widows, the unlovely and those who were openly antagonistic and complacent about spiritual things. In thus doing so they built relationships with the people and they earned the opportunity to tell them the good news of the gospel and how it transforms lives.

Reflecting on the past, and on the poor woman's answer to Rev William Ross, the question is posed, "should there be a recovery of evangelical social engagement" as exemplified by the work of the Sisters of the People.

In trying to answer this, we need to think about what is the relationship of evangelism to social engagement, is each of similar importance or does one take precedence over the other?.

On the MLJ website(www.mljtrust.org) there are recordings of interviews Dr Martyn Lloyd-Jones had participated in. One is with Aneirin Talfan Davies on the BBC in 1968 and the other with Joan Bakewell in 1970. In both these interviews, Dr Martyn Lloyd-Jones is questioned on the relationship of preaching of the gospel to social engagement. Dr Martyn Lloyd-Jones gives a very clear answer;

> "It is the Evangelical gospel and it's preaching that has the greatest impact socially. He emphasised the priority of the Evangelical gospel. The gospel is the power of God unto salvation. Romans Ch 1, v16 and all follows from it. Gospel first, then changed hearts can change the world."

In Victorian times, there were many examples of evangelical zeal resulting in social ministry.

William Booth the founded of the Salvation Army and it's great work amongst the poor.

Charles H Spurgeon organised free schools for destitute children, advocated for the abolition of slavery, established orphanages and cared for widows. Spurgeon created 66 parachurch ministries to care for London's social ills. However, his evangelical activism was more than a social program. It was a transformative force that created a recognisable difference.

In 1866, Spurgeon called his church to action by stating "Dear friends, we are a huge church, and should be doing more for the Lord in this great city." [3]

Yet despite all of Spurgeon's altruism, his biggest accolade was that he was the 'Prince of Preachers'.

Lord Shaftesbury was a Christian who worked tirelessly to improve the lives of the poor.

It was also a time of unprecedented opportunities for women to participate in social ministry.

Josephine Butler fought against prostitution and human trafficking.

The Quaker Elizabeth Fry worked hard for prison reform. She was the driving force behind new legislation to improve the treatment of prisoners, especially women prisoners. She was instrumental in the 1823 Goal Act, which stipulated sex segregation of prisoners and female warders for women prisoners, which protected them from sexual exploitation. She also funded a prison school for children imprisoned with their mothers. Elizabeth Fry's work was outstanding, groundbreaking and inspiring.

Catherine Booth the cofounder of the Salvation Army was a street preacher and had a great heart for the poor. She was known as the 'Mother of the Salvation Army' and she shared her husband's passionate belief in the need for reform of the church's outreach to the unsaved. Catherine firmly believed in the potential of female ministry as a powerful tool to reach the unsaved masses. Catherine Booth is also remembered for her steadfast commitment to waging war on poverty and injustice.

Now coming back to our question, "should there be a recovery of evangelical social engagement?" Perhaps we could look at a modern-day example in detail in an attempt to unpack an answer to this question.

Pastor John Funnell ministers at Noddfa Church, Abersychan, South Wales. [4] It is an area of intense poverty. The comprehensive school is the second highest in Wales and double the national average for free school meals, 72% of the young people in the comprehensive school are from single parent families. There is an ingrained benefit culture, with fourth and fifth generation unemployed. The community has suffered since the mines closed, and people feel isolated with no hope.

Yet there is a good community spirit, and so much talent and people haven't had an opportunity

Pastor John started his work eight years ago, in a church of six attendees and with closure imminent. He knocked on every door to introduce himself, and he wrote a letter saying that he was there to serve and gave contact details if any wanted help or just a chat. He met with open hostility, as it's a tight knit community who have seen lots of people come and go over the years. Pastor John analysed the situation in Abersychan and says there are three lies the culture tells the people of this community.

(i) you are good enough the way you are;
(ii) you can be anything you want to be;
(iii) nothing is your fault.

That sums up the message from the world.

Pastor John says, firstly the young people of the valley know that they are not good enough. They are addicted to various things, have children from several relationships, spent most of their lives unemployed, on anti-depressants and can't reconcile this message from the world with who they know themselves to be.

However, it is the message of the Gospel that produces truth and speaks powerfully into their situation;

> Gospel truth says you are not good enough, you are a broken sinful wretch And when there is honesty about this gospel truth, and there is repentance, then a great blessing of salvation is imparted.

Secondly, the world says, "you can be anything you want to be". This sounds lovely, but it's not possible. In the Abersychan community instead of the positive social markers, job, home, car, bank account etc, they look for negative social markers; how many cars have I stolen, how many drugs have I taken, who have I beaten up?

Then the Gospel declares truth powerfully into this situation.

Gospel truth says you can't be anything you want to be, but you can be a new creation in Christ and He can give your life meaning and purpose.

Thirdly the world says, "nothing is your fault". Your Dad was a heroin addict, so you're a heroin addict, your Mum neglected you, so you neglect your kids.

The Gospel declares truth powerfully into this situation.

Gospel truth says No! Take ownership, stop using your past, to make wrong decisions today. You can have a fresh start in Jesus, follow Him, He transforms lives.

So that is how Pastor John attacks the culture, with the truth of the Gospel and that truth is what's drawing people in.

Pastor John says, it is far from a social gospel, but we do practice what we preach. Jesus highlighted the two greatest commandments – love your God and love your neighbour and that's exactly what we do. Pastor John says our focus is on being incarnational, actively being around people and bringing Christ to them through whatever means we can.

A working definition of incarnational ministry is "the immersion of oneself into a local culture and showing Christlikeness to that culture". Incarnational ministry seeks to dispense with ministry 'from a distance' and embraces ministry 'up close and personal' – the love of God and the Gospel of Christ embodied by the person ministering.

The ministry at Noddfa is always driven and supported by the Word of God. Jesus is the answer to all our problems but you can't force it on people. You need a relationship with the people in the community, to apply the Gospel in a way that is relevant, in a way that they can grasp.

The church finds out the needs of the community and we endeavour by all ways and means to show the love and compassion of Christ. The church finds out the needs of the community from the local Council and from the schools, in order to meet needs with Christ. This gives many points of engagement.

One outreach involves helping a local secular charity for teen Mum's (teaching them to cook, clean and be Mums)

In the church they offer homework clubs and tutoring sessions, and music lessons, and youth outreach work.

They feed the homeless and have a Food Bank 4 days a week.

The church is open everyday and everything is free.

There have been wonderful evidence of the Gospel radically transforming lives in Abersychan. Noddfa Church at Abersychan has grown from 6 to 200 people attending in 8 years.

Here is one wonderful testimony from Abersychan to the transforming power of the gospel. Pastor John states;

> "Alex, I've taken him under my wing, he's got a gift for preaching, incredibly studious. He's in his mid-30s and come to us at the beginning of Covid when the church was shut. I was doing "Fire meetings" for men in my garden, whilst staying within the Covid regulations. Someone brought Alex to the meeting. He barely said anything and he had a right attitude on him. He had just come out after several years in prison and I asked him what for and he said heroin and violence."

Jesus met with him and we're a few years on now and he's training with me and he's a joy. We have 12 men in the church who are in some development who will eventually be sent out.

What an amazing example of the Gospel being the power of God unto salvation and lives being transformed by the Gospel.

John Stott in his book 'The Cross of Christ' says

"The cross calls us to a much more radical and costly kind of evangelism than most churches have begun to consider, let alone experience. The cross calls us to social action too, because it summons us to the imitation of Christ" [5]

Justin Holcombe on the Gospel Coalition website says:

"Proclaiming the good news of Christ's saving work should be accompanied by tangible acts of love, service and mercy towards our neighbours if the Gospel message is to be recognised in its full power" [5a]

Tim Keller in his book "The call of the Jericho Road" says

"The ministry of mercy is not just a means to an end in evangelism. Word and deed are equally necessary, mutually interdependent and inseparable ministries, each carried out with the single purpose of the spread of the Kingdom of God" [6]

So in the light of all this, should there be a recovery of evangelical social engagement.

If we look at the public ministry of the Lord Jesus Christ, He not only preached the good news of salvation, calling mankind to repentance, but He also fed the hungry and healed the sick.

If we let scripture have the last word, the scriptures summon Christians to, "love thy neighbour" (Mark 12 v 31) to "do good to all" (Galatians 6 v 10) and to be "a people zealous of good works" (Titus 2 c 14)

Our dear Sisters of the People who were such exemplars of an effective incarnational ministry. They immersed themselves into the local cultures of abject poverty, hostility, drunkenness, indifference to spiritual needs and so very much more so that they could show Christlikeness and the love of Christ to these people and share the good news of the Gospel with them.

"For I was hungry and you gave me food; I was thirsty and you gave me drink; I was a stranger and you took me in, I was naked and you clothed me, I was sick and you visited me, I was in prison and you came to me"

…………in as much as you did it to the least of these My brethren, you did it to Me.

Matthew Ch 25 v 35, 36, 40 NKJV

Ian Shaw in his book "Evangelicals and Social Action" concludes that

"The combination of evangelisation of the lost and compassionate care of the needy has been stitched into the regenerated DNA of evangelical believers" [7]

Well that was undoubtedly true of our Sisters of the People. May we be deeply challenged by their story, to a reappraisal of our own walk, witness and work for the Lord.

Our dear Sisters of the People have received their accolade and their reward **"Well done good and faithful servants……enter into the joy of your Lord"**

<><><><><><>

<><><><>

Index of Sisters of the People 1903 – 1993

Page Reference

AVERY, E K	67
CHURCH	12, 16-17
CARTER, Rose	12
DAVIES, Mair	82
DAVIS, Elizabeth Ann	82
DAVIES, Jean E	82
DAVIES, Gertrude	10
DOWBER, Joyce	77-80
EVANS, Annie	58
FRANCIS, Esther	57,92
GRIFFITHS, Moreena	74
HAYES, Margaret	77,81
HILL	12
HUGHES, C A	46,47
HOLE, Elsie	59-60,81,91
JOHN, Priscilla Mary	82
JONES, Alison	12, 15-16,20, 56, 81, 89-90
JONES, Elizabeth	66
JONES, Heulwen	78,81,88, 95-97
JONES, Kate	74, 87-88,91
JONES, Mair	66,81
JONES, Margaret	54,66, 97-98
JONES, Martha	21-31
JONES, Sarah	10
LEWIS, Lydia	55
LEWIS-EVANS, Mavis	82
LLOYD, L M	10-11, 33
MARKEY, May	76
MORROW, Gwen	67,73,81

Page Reference

PARFITT, Ruth	82
PIERCE	44
POPE, Thelma	66
REES, Gladys	10
ROBERTS, Emily	67-72
ROBERTS, Janet	38
ROOK, Ruby	82
THOMAS, May	12
THOMAS, Morwen	74-75
TOLLEY, Joan	80
WALKER, Eileen	12
WALKER, Kathleen	75-76, 81
WATKINS, Ellen	33, 60-61, 92-95
WHITE	58
WILLIAMS, Beatrice	66
WILLIAMS, Elsie	38
WILLIAMS, Mary	67, 76-77

References

Chapter One – Early Beginnings

(1)   Howell Williams, The Romance of the Forward Movement, Page 159
(2)   Christian Standard July 1891
(3)   Christian Standard January 1892
(4)   Atgofion am y John Pugh, chapter 7, Pages 37-38 (private translation)
(5)   Dorothea Price-Hughes, The Life of Hugh Price-Jones
(6)   Monthly Treasury, August 1894
(7)   Atgofion am y John Pugh, Pages 37-38 (private translation)
(8)   Howell Williams, The Romance of the Forward Movement, Pages 159-160

Chapter Two – Early Days of the Sisters of the People

(1)   The Torch, January 1909
(2)   The Torch, March 1905
(3)   The Torch, January 1906
(4)   The Torch, December 1906
(5)   The Torch, January 1908
(6)   The Torch, January 1908
(7)   The Torch, November 1910
(8)   Atgofion am y John Pugh, Pages 51-52 (private translation)
(9)   Y Goleuad, December 1908
(10) The Torch, September 1906
(11) The Torch, August 1909
(12) The Torch, March 1907
(13) The Torch, February 1907
(14) The Torch, March 1909
(15) The Treasury, Vol. 1, No. 7, July 1913
(16) The Treasury, Vol. 1, No.7, May 1913
(17) The Torch, February 1906

Chapter Three – Slum Stories from the Diary of Sister Martha Jones

(1) Slum stories from the Diary of Sister Martha Jones
     The Torch, Feb/April/May 1910

Chapter Four – Treborth Preventative Home

(1)   The Torch, November 1905
(2)   The Torch, January 1906
(2a) The Torch, February 1906
(3)   The Torch, March 1907
(4)   The Torch, May 1908
(4a) The Torch, December 1907

Chapter Five – Kingswood Treborth Rescue and Preventative Home

(5)   South Wales Daily News, 8th May 1908
(6)   The Torch, May 1909
(7)   The Torch, October 1910
(8)   The Treasury, August 1908
(8a)   The Treasury, September 1915
(9)   The Treasury, April 1938
(10)   Thomson Weekly News, 10th October 1925
       Western Mail, 5th October 1925
(11)   Christchurch Times, 26th July 1913
(12)   The Treasury, June 1931
(13)   The Treasury, November 1935
(13a) The Treasury, February 1939
(14)   The Treasury, September 1941
(14a) The Treasury, February 1942
(15)   The Treasury, June 1947
(16)   The Treasury, September 1947

Chapter Six – Helps and Hinderances

(1)   The Torch, June 1905
(2)   The Treasury, November 1914
(3)   The Treasury, January 1914
(4)   The Treasury, April 1916
(5)   The Treasury, April 1920
(6)   The Treasury, May 1928
(6a)   The Treasury, June 1930
(7)   The Treasury, August 1936

Chapter Seven- Blood, Sweat, Toil and Tears – Sisters Reports from the Inter-War Years

(8)   The Treasury, April 1924
(9)   The Treasury, April 1924
(9a)   The Treasury March 1924
(10)   The Treasury, March 1924
(10a)   The Treasury, August 1920
(11)   The Treasury, April 1924
(12)   The Treasury, September 1930
(13)   The Treasury, April 1933
(14)   The Treasury, April 1935

Chapter Eight – A New Vision for a New Era

(1)   The Treasury, July 1947
(2)   The Treasury, February 1948
(2a)   The Treasury, May 1967
(3)   The Treasury, August 1952
(4)   The Treasury, April 1955
(4a)   "Home Mission News Sheet" April 1959

Chapter Nine – New Beginnings, North Wales

(5)   The Torch, October 1908
(6)   The Treasury, October 1953
(7)   The Treasury, July 1960
(8)   The Treasury, January 1961
(9)   The Treasury, Jan 1964
(10)   The Treasury, June 1960
(11)   The Treasury, February 1946
(14)   The Treasury, April 1967
(15)   The Treasury, July 1946
(16)   The Treasury, April 1955
(17)   The Treasury, October 1955
(18a) The Treasury, September 1965
(18b) Liverpool Daily Post, Welsh Edition, 23/3/1964
(19)   Glad Tidings, April 1968

Chapter Ten – New Beginnings, South Wales

(20)   The Treasury, March 1948
(21)   The Treasury, September 1949
(22)   The Treasury, March 1955
(23)   The Treasury, June 1959
(24)   The Treasury, September 1949
(25)   The Treasury, February 1950
(26)   The Treasury, February/March 1952
(27)   The Treasury, March 1953
(28)   The Treasury, June 1955
(29)   The Treasury, July 1952
(30)   The Treasury, March 1957
(31)   The Treasury, May 1961
(32)   The Treasury, December 1962
(33)   The Treasury, November 1950
(34)   The Treasury, August 1951
(35)   The Treasury, September 1954
(36)   The Treasury, September 1955
(37)   The Treasury, Sept 1964

(38)   The Treasury, October 1952
(39)   The Treasury, Sept 1964
(40)   The Treasury, April 1956
(41)   The Treasury, March 1960
(42)   The Treasury, December 1956
(43)   The Treasury, November 1960
(44)   The Treasury, February 1960
(45)   The Treasury, January 1961
(46)   Calvinistic Methodist Archive AZ3/413 – Gabalfa
(47)   The Treasury, March 1967
(48)   The Treasury, October 1967
(49)   The Treasury, October 2020 – Tribute to Mrs Joyce Akrill
(50)   The Treasury, December 1960
(51)   The Treasury, September 1961

Chapter Eleven – Warts and all

(1)   The Torch, February 1906
(2)   The Torch, July 1906
(3)   The Torch July 1909
(4)   Calvinistic Methodist Archive AZ3/751
(4a)   The Torch, October 1908
(5)   The Torch, May 1905
(6)   The Treasury, April 1921
(7)   The Treasury, January 1957
(8)   The Torch, February 1907
(9)   The Torch, April 1907
(10)   The Romance of the Forward Movement, Page 168
(10a) The Treasury, June and November 1967
(11)   The Treasury, September 1968

Chapter Twelve – Long Serving Sisters of the People

(1)   The Treasury, June 1957
(2)   Calvinistic Methodist Archive AZ3/751
(3)   Calvinistic Methodist Archive AZ3/408
(4)   The Treasury, December 1966

(5)   The Treasury, July 1943
(6)   The Treasury, May 1954
(7)   The Treasury, November 1980
(8)   The Treasury, February 1946
(9)   The Treasury, August 1949

Chapter Thirteen – Champions of the Cause

(1)   Romance of the Forward Movement, Pages 164-165
(2)   The Monthly Treasury, VIII/I, 1920
(3)   Atgofion am y John Pugh, Page 14 (private translation)
(4)   The Torch, April 1907
(5)   The Treasury, April 1931
(5a)   The Treasury, May 1964
(6)   Christian Standard, November 1892
(7)   The Romance of the Forward Movement, Pages 85-86
(8)   'The transmutation of wealth', Alliance Witness, October 8, 1958

Chapter Fourteen – What Shall We Say to These things?

(1)   Atogofion am y John Pugh by Annie Pugh-Williams (private translation)
(2)   Seeking God's Kingdom – The Non-conformists Social Gospel in Wales 1906-1939, Robert Pope
(3)   Spurgeon's Autobiography, 3:168
(4)   An interview with Pastor John Funnel on "Emerging Stories Podcast," ES10
(5)   The Cross of Christ, John Stott
(5a)   Thegospelcoalition.org "Why the Rising Social Awareness in the Church Should Encourage Us," May 15, 2013, Justin Holcomb
(6)   The call of the Jericho Road, Tim Keller
(7)   Evangelicals and Social Action, Ian Shaw

Bibliography

- Grace, grit and gumption, Geraint Fielder
- The Presbyterian Church of Wales (Calvinistic Methodists Historical Handbook 1735-1905), Edward Griffiths
- The History of Welsh Calvinistic Methodism III : Growth and Consolidation c 1814-1914, John Gwynfor Jones
- Cardiff's Temples of Faith : A Thousand Years of Places of Worship, John B Hilling
- The Span of the Cross : Christian Religion and Society in Wales 1914-2000, Densil D Morgan
- The Religious History of Wales : Religious Life and Practice in Wales from the Seventeenth Century to the Present Day, Richard C Allen
- Faith and Crisis of a Nation : Wales 1890-1914, Tudur R Jones
- Creative Fellowship : An Outline of the History of Calvinistic Methodism in Wales, Morgan Watcyn-Williams
- Voices from the Past : History of English Conference of the Presbyterian Church of Wales 1889-1938, R Buick Knox
- Seeking God's Kingdom : The Non-conformist Social Gospel in Wales 1906-1939, Robert Pope
- The Romance of the Forward Movement, Howell Williams
- Atgofion am John Pugh, Annie Pugh-Williams (private translation)
- Glamorgan Christianity, in 1905-06, R Tudor Jones
  A statistical survey – Glamorgan County History Vol VI Pg 254
- Carriers of the Fire – The women of the Welsh Revival 1904-5 Karen Lowe
- The Welsh Revival (1904-5) Recovering the role of the Welsh women. Sarah Louise Prendergast (PhD thesis 2018)
- The Forward Movement of the Presbyterian Church of Wales 1890-1914 Chiefly in Cardiff, Maureen Wise, (MA thesis 1993)

Printed in Great Britain
by Amazon